BAHGOD

BahGod

Lukas Allen

Lukas Allen

Contents

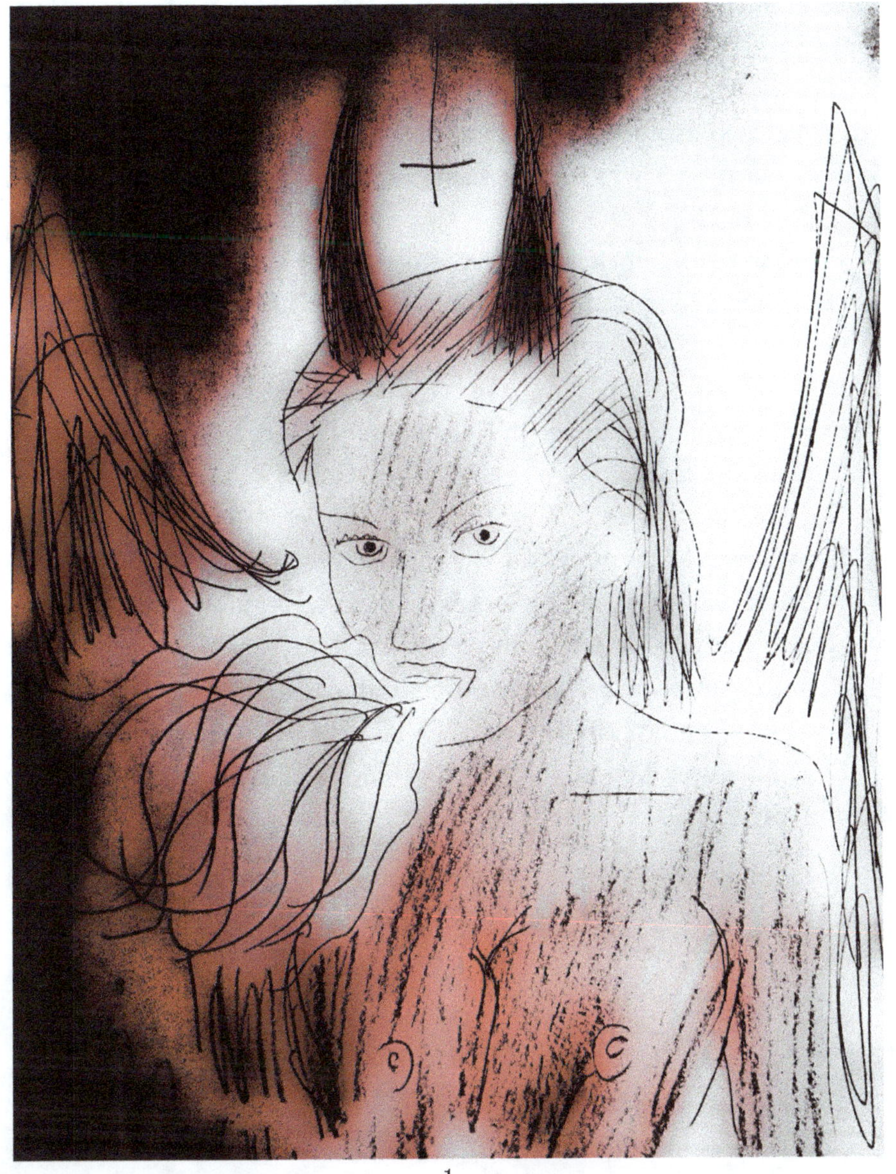

I have seen her, as I store into yeh mirror… I have seen her before my very own eyes. She is Hell incarnate! Her eyes blaze with fires of thousands of burning sausages! SAUSAGES!! What did those sausages do to her, yeh ask?

I know what they did. They tore back their grace from God, those sausages broke from their fear, and were cast into the mortal abyss for on ever eternity. There be no escape for those sausages, in her heathen eyes.

Fear the eternal maker!! Fear him, yelse this she beast will claim you as well… like sausages…

God, I think I'm getting hungry. Please drop me a sausage from Heaven, yeh ask.

But there ain't no sausage in Hell. There is not even some pork rinds. Only death and fire.

Not even death!

For yeh will be tortured, slowly, roasted over a pit of fire on a stick…

But look yeh now, at her eternal, immortal figure. Look yeh now, and tremble at what MAY await you, if you do not fry your sausages just right, just crispy enough, while sealing in the inner juices…

Look now, and tremble on the DEVIL'S DAUGHTER!!!!

For I have seen her as well, blowing smoke in my eyes as I store into the mirror.

2

Tobacco is bad. Why? Because it's bad for you. It will kill you slowly, with no chance of repentance, when you brace a fat cigar on your lips…

This is to the man named Joe, a heathen amongst mortals, albeit a just man. Heathen… because of his insatiable lust for a fat Cuban cigar.

Well, I see yeh now, and I see you 'ave one fate, other than eternal damnation.

You look at the cigar, contemplating your own suicide, like a bullet to the lungs, it will hit you. You look at yeh cigar, and you see only utter black tar torture.

But there is one path of redemption.

Drop the cigar, and pick up the plough. For none shall heed your glorious change if yeh work on God's green earth.

But yeh ask, what plant shalt I useth?

Tobacco.

AHAH! There you see! It is immortally part of the loop! You will never escape from your valid interdiction! For yeh grow it yourself on your fields. The master has become the servant, to this most foul, unholy, villainous, albeit very smooth and fine on the tongue, vilest of all plants.

Watch yeh now, for the Daughter of the Devil does not smoke tobacco. She smokes your soul.

Look yeh now, as she rolls the finely loose paper around you… making a big fat cigar…

And smokes your soul, after you take your final puff.

Beware your credence in tobacco!

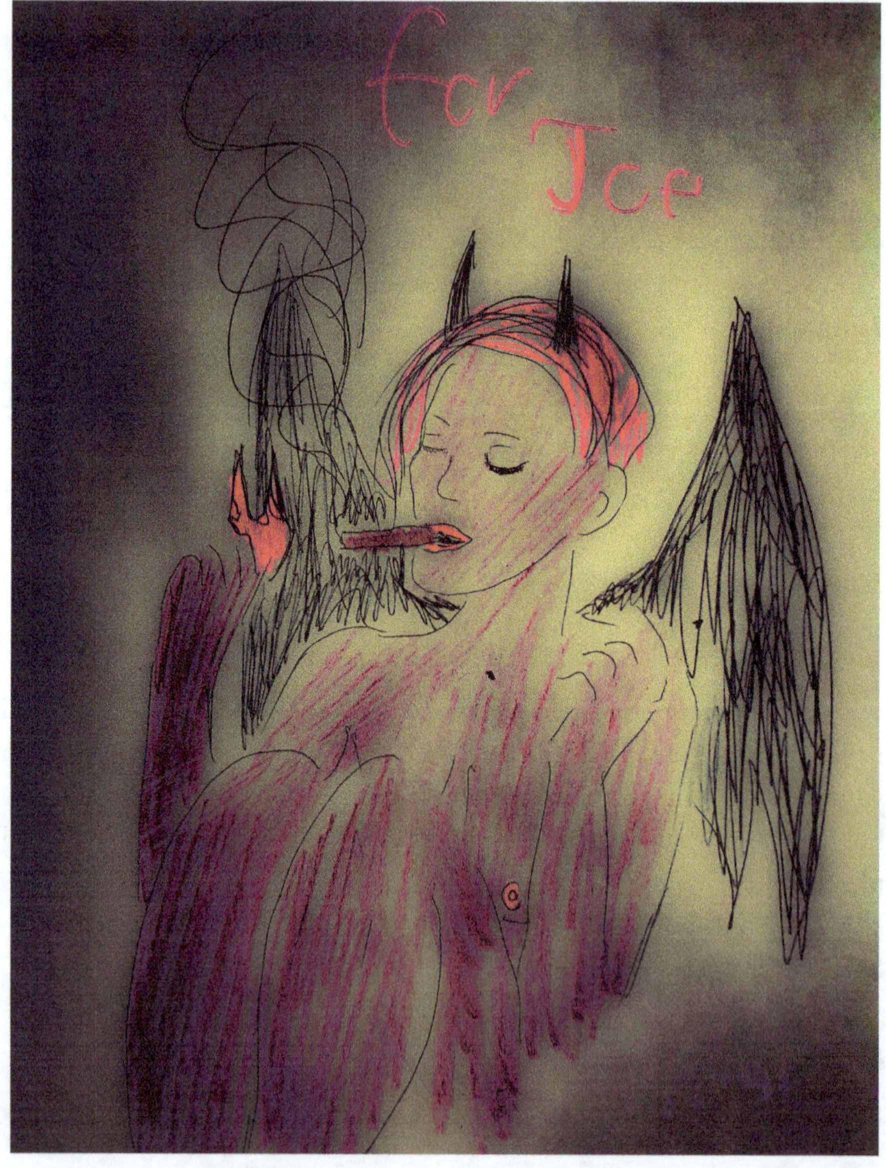

3

And yeh alcohol. Yeh drink wine like blood, like the vampyr, like the Devil's Daughter. You take the blood of your countrymen upon your lips, even other countrymen, and drink the fruits of their labor, in a glass of wine.

The intoxication is what Hell feels like! No... the day after is what Hell feels like! But like, worse! It is always worse down below...

And you shalt see it yourself, if yeh do not put down that glass of wine.

For the Devil's Daughter drinks blood like wine!

All of our blood!

We shalt see, as the endless loop of intoxication happens again. We shalt see, as I explain.

For you get up, feel drowsy and hungover, and start the cycle anew in the evening. There is never an end to the horrible intoxication! And what tis worse is the actions you partake while drunk!!

You fight, become less than animals in your own blessed home. You make love, and do not remember your partner. You kill, when you have driveth down the road.

You kill, and then you have lost your soul to the Devil's Daughter.

There is no path out of intoxication. For the pangs and cravings are ever so present...

But there is hope. Put down the glass of wine, the bottle of booze, and do not kill, and most especially do not driveth down the road.

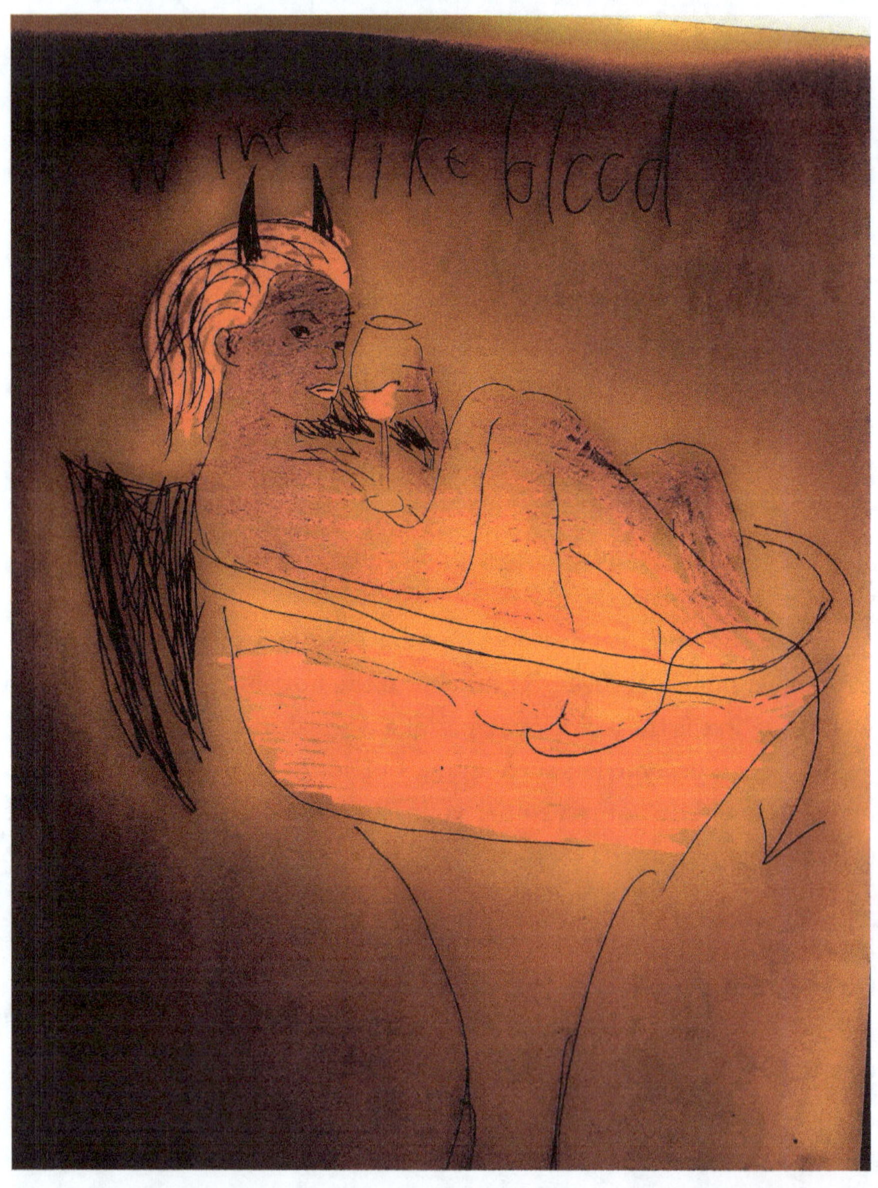
wine like blood

4

And now we get to the heart of immortal sin. Nudity.

Yes, I shalt draweth the terror down in her natural form… but that's only how I see her! She is completely, sinfully, shamelessly unclothe! It is madness on my blessed eyes, looking on her sweet, lithe figure-

I mean, it is temptation! It is awful!

She is trying to bring my soul to Hell with nudity! I see her, baring her fangs at me, smiling for she has another in her grasp already… ME!!

I do this not to only save you. I wish to save all, and all happens to include myself.

And the Daughter of the Devil wishes to claim all.

With horrible, unbridled, monstrously seductive nudity!!

She is tempting me now, flying above me in my soul… Haunting my every tempted keystroke. Every letter shapes and forms into her own naked image!!

Is there any way out of this madness? I ask yeh this, shalt my soul be saved from… nudity?

I must clothe myself. I must put on layers and layers to protect against the cold and watchful eyes! At least *I*… will not be so nude.

I will draw her again, to capture her evil malevolence, and bring it forth to the light of the Lord.

Yeh shall see, that nudity is SIN!!

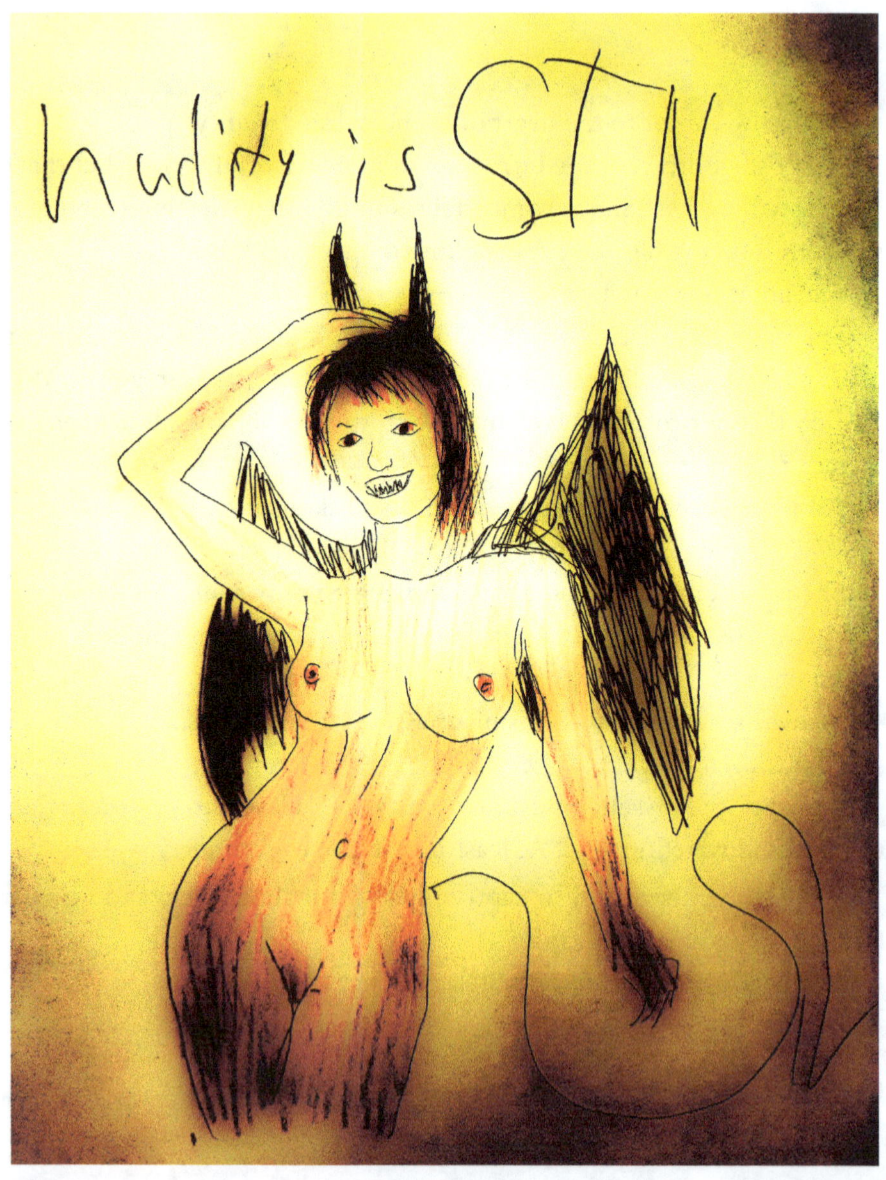
nudity is SIN

5

There ist one place nudity may be looked upon finely, plainly, and that ist with another in the blessed confines of marriage.

Of course, it is fine if they are different race, even same sex! There is no bounds to love!

Except in holy marriage.

For if yeh do not marry, yeh shall see your nudity marred and unholified, like rotten swiss cheese.

Yeh shall see your love unclothed, and wonder who or what that thing is.

You shall be making love to the Devil's Daughter, if you do not love in holy matrimony.

Repent! Fear the blasted nudity! For she lifts her skirt up, tempting the young and foolish into breaking their word to the Father. They go willingly into her open maws!!

Repent! Do not go into her tracts and ducts and swooshes! They may be the last swoosh you ever get! A swoosh in the lower regions, and yet yeh shall see it will all be over.

Disease will riven your figure! Will corrupt your mind after lust! I speaketh truth and the Lord's will!

Do not ever break the binds of matrimony, elst yeh be makin' love to the Devil's Daughter.

Sex is sacred!

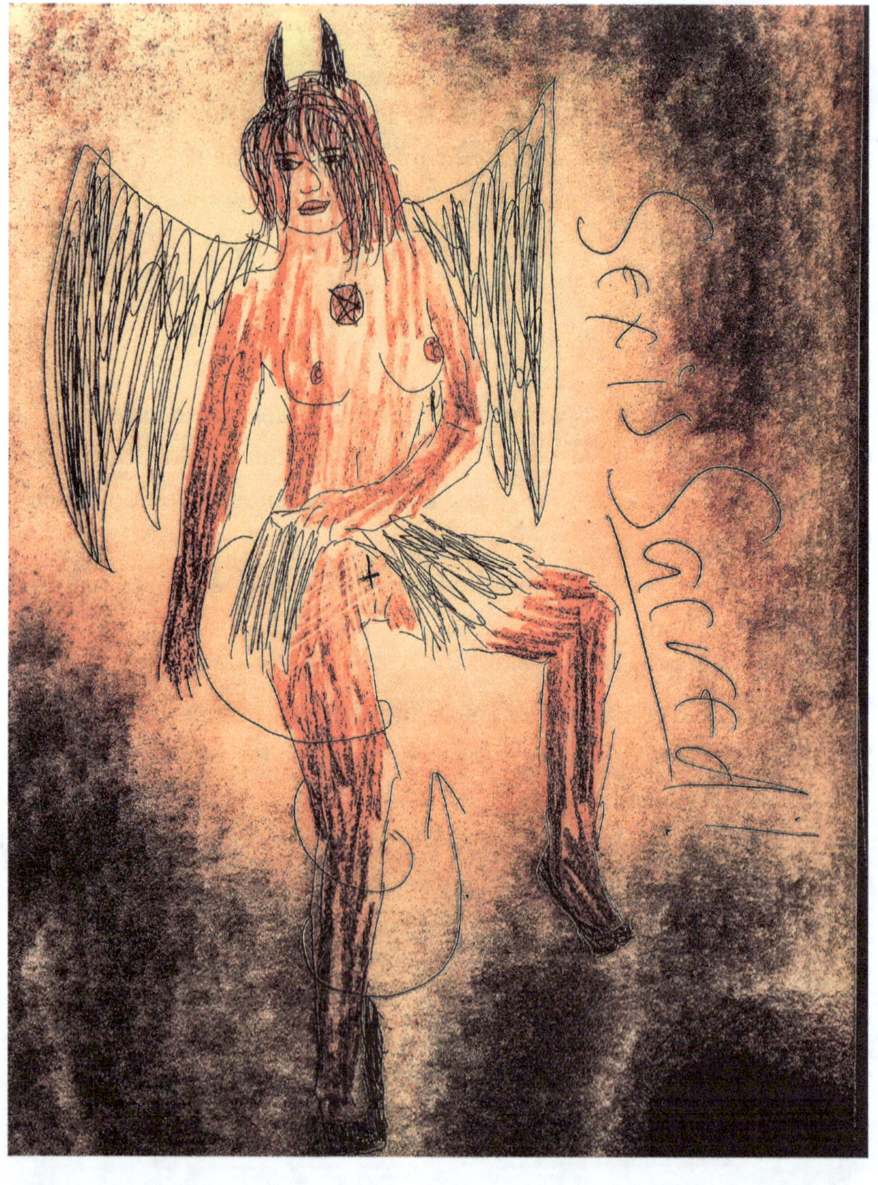
Sex is Sacred!

6

MAHGOD.

I have seen her in the liveth world, tempting the purest of all. I have seen her walk down the street in holy malevolence, smiling and waving to every pure virgin and nice old lady... I have seeneth her stalk the very lands.

But what was she doing?

She was getting groceries.

This flabberghasts me... for I do not understand how something so normal as getting groceries could be a sin.

For that is what it must be!! For the Devil's Daughter gets groceries amongst us!!

Hmm... I shall have to abstain from getting groceries from now on... What- No, I can't eat that... OR that... This pencil tastes a bit funny, so I can't eat that...

No matter. Maybe I shall get my neighbor to get me groceries-

HEARKEN!! I have become the seducer of minds and souls!! I verily wish to make others sin for me!! This is madness. I cannot allow another to get my own groceries. For groceries are... evil?

I shall take to the streets. I shall live like a natural martyr and hermit, for you, dear soul. For you.

I shall defy the Devil's Daughter!

No matter her sweet temptation, an' her nice smile and wave with all that groceries...

God, I am hungry. Please drop me a sausage.

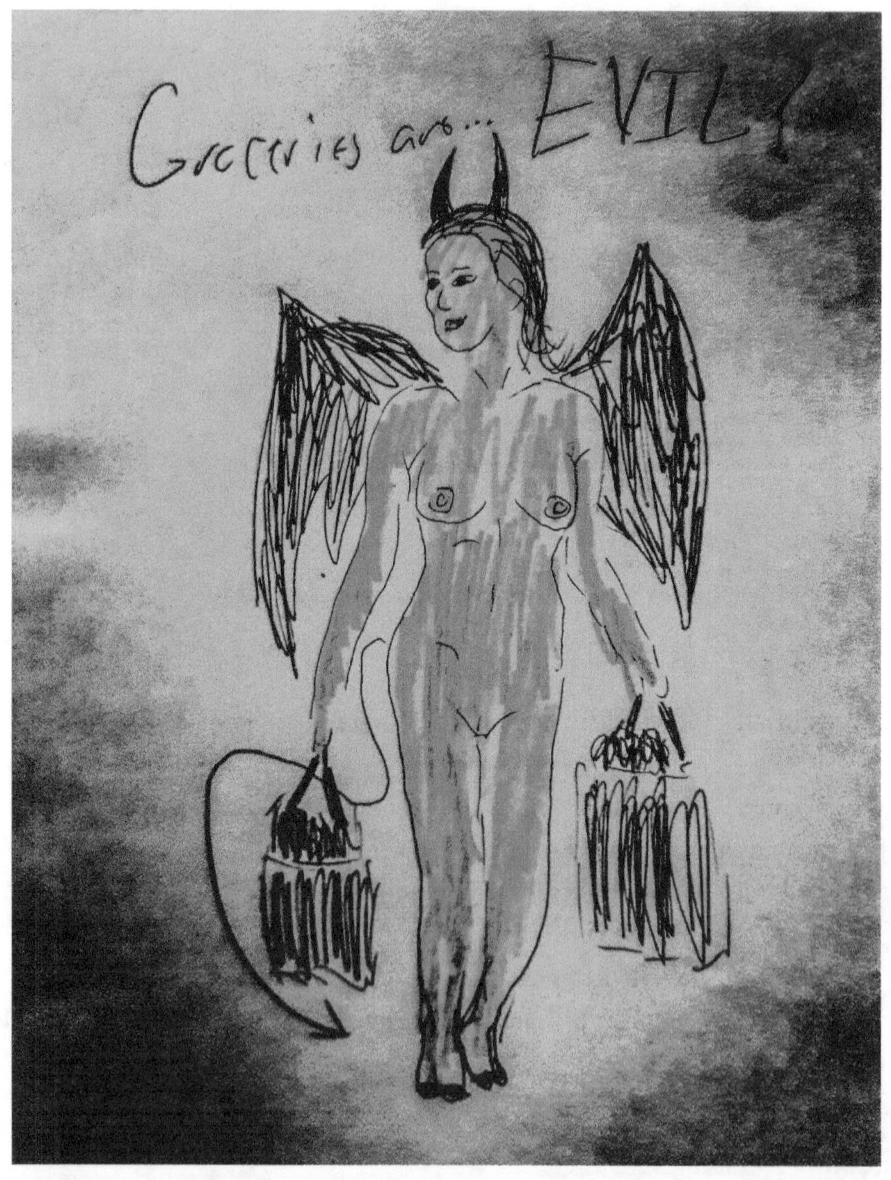
Groceries are... EVIL?

7

———

"Would you like to get a coffee?"

She asketh this, as I try to pick up my breakfast from crumbs in the street. The harlotrous she beast tempts me now.

"I mean, I just am really lonely ever since I moved here, and you seem you know what's hip and happening! Ha ha..." she said rubbing an arm in feign nervousness. Really I see her now, snapping her maws in hunger for my soul, under the guise of a cute, polite smile...

"I sayeth this, demon of Hell, you shall never get my soul, and I shall stand forth from the storm of your never ending lust for God's lives." I said, crossing my arms.

She looked surprised, and said, *"...I'll pay? We can get pastries?"*

My stomach grumbled, and I said, "I shall take your pastry upon the brow, rather than be brought low. But I accept your evil temptation, and I shall show you I will not be tempted, by only drinking a coffee."

She smiled, and said, *"Great! You're just kinda cute, is all. I was so nervous even coming over here! Let's go, let's go!"* and she clenched my arm in hers and dragged me with the might of Hell to the coffee shop.

I had won this battle, I knew this. I knew this by drinking my black coffee, that the Devil's Daughter shalt never claim my soul.

She looked into my eyes, staring into my soul as she drank, and I knew she was planning her next assault.

I shall remain ever vigilant... with coffee!!

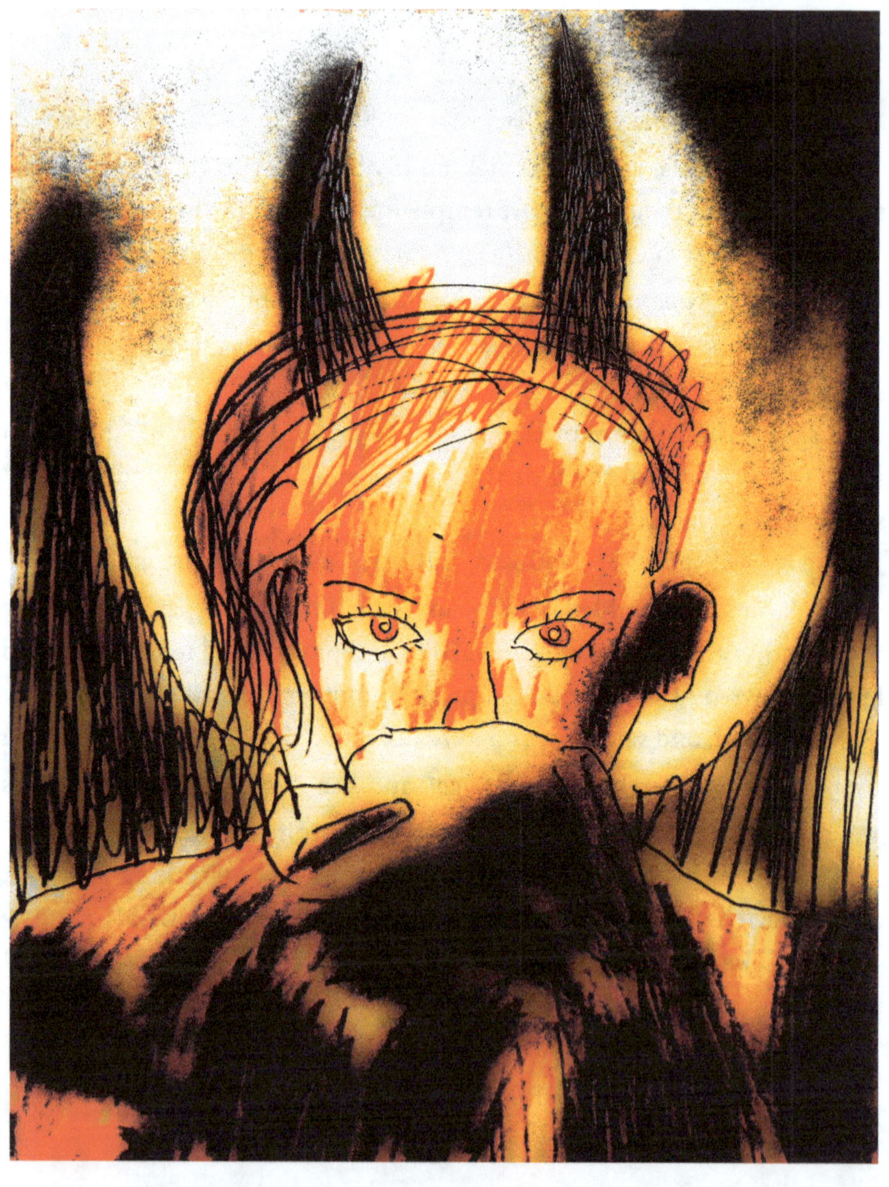

8

I am awake, I am vigilant. I am awake, I am vigilant...

The rats scamper across my bedsheets, as I cannot sleep. The fleas nip at my legs, as I writhe in maddened woke.

I see this evil she beast, down the street, from my window!! She is partying and laughing with men, women, and all manner of sorts! Bringing their souls to HELL one step at a time!

I must drink more coffee... I must remain woke...

I shouted out to the partygoers in the street.

"REPENT!!" I yelled.

"Up yours!" one of the men said. Poor child, he does not know that the Devil's Daughter has her arm around his waist.

She looked sadly up at me, and left his side.

She cometh now, knocking on my door.

She sayeth this, as I open on only a crack.

"You wanna go out with us? You seem pretty lively!" she said.

"I shalt save the other souls you have seduced! I must! I will! I shalt!" I sayeth, "But I need more coffee. I must stay vigilant against... *you,* vile she beast."

"...Maybe you need a beer to mellow out?" she said, looking so cute and innocent... It is all a lie!!

I drank a non alcoholic beverage, as she *agreed* with me about my points on this group's sinful habits in the evening. In the end it was only me and her...

I knew she wanted her prey alone, as she smiled so sweetly.

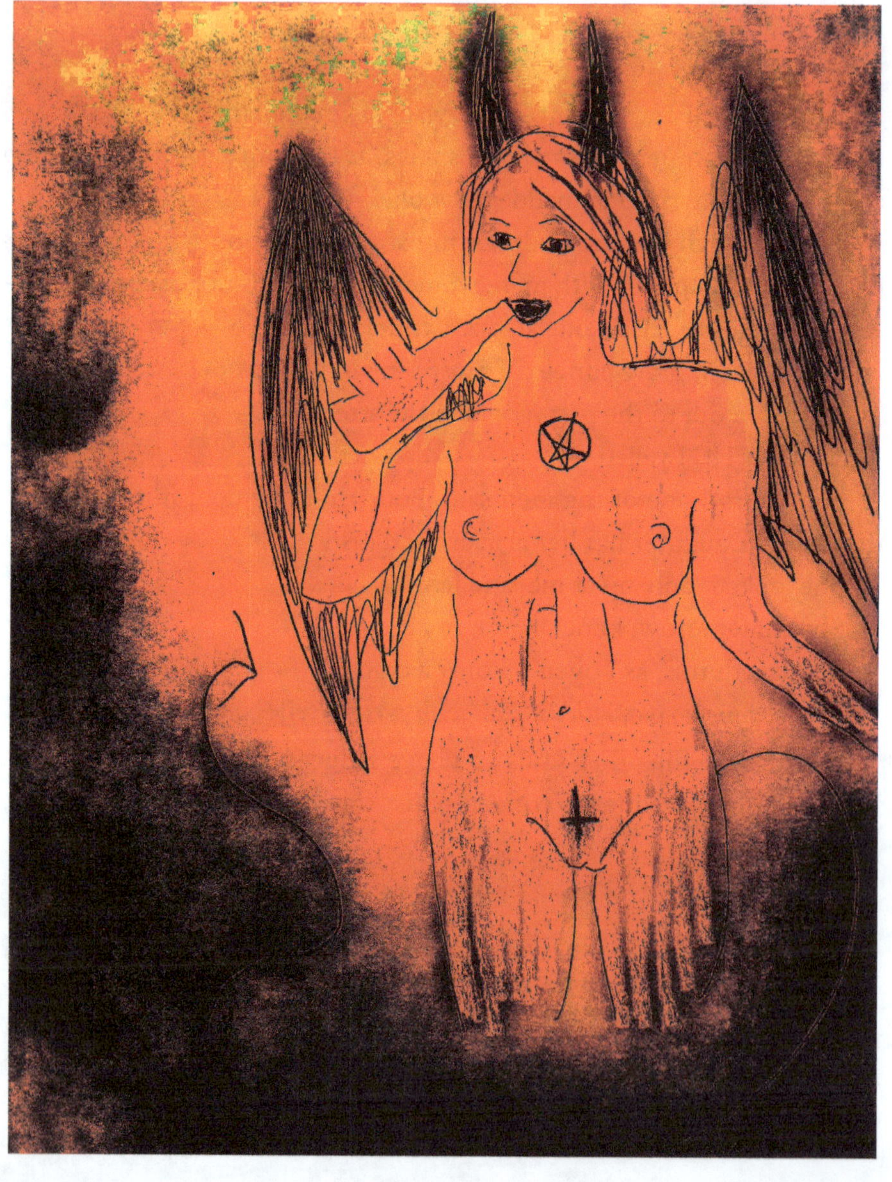

9

_____

"*What are you doing?*" she asketh me, as I blew God's trombone in the street in the morning.

"Do you not see I am blowing my horn for the gates of Heaven?? The time is nigh! The people *must* repent!! Revelations is upon us! Jesus will come down from above, smite the unbelievers, and kill you all if you do not listen to this sweet melody!" I said, first shouting at her, then other passersby.

"*...You wanna play with me??*" she said.

"I shalt never lay myself low by playing with a naked she beast's body-" I said.

"*I meant instruments. Just because I walk around naked all the time doesn't mean I want every sucker down there. I play guitar!*" she said, smiling nicely.

Guitar. Of course. The most evilest of instruments. None are more beautiful than a good trombone, played by me, like a seraph of Heaven singing...

I followed her to her studio apartment, trombone safely by my side, and watched her take something out of a case.

She cradled the wretched instrument of the Devil, verily said, "*Was my dad's. He gave it to me so I have something to remember him by.*"

I played against her vile melody, as she smiled and rocked and rolled, puffing and huffing my trombone.

I knoweth other guitar players, and I know their souls are on the brink as well, for the Devil's Daughter plays your strings.

For Dylan, may you repent.

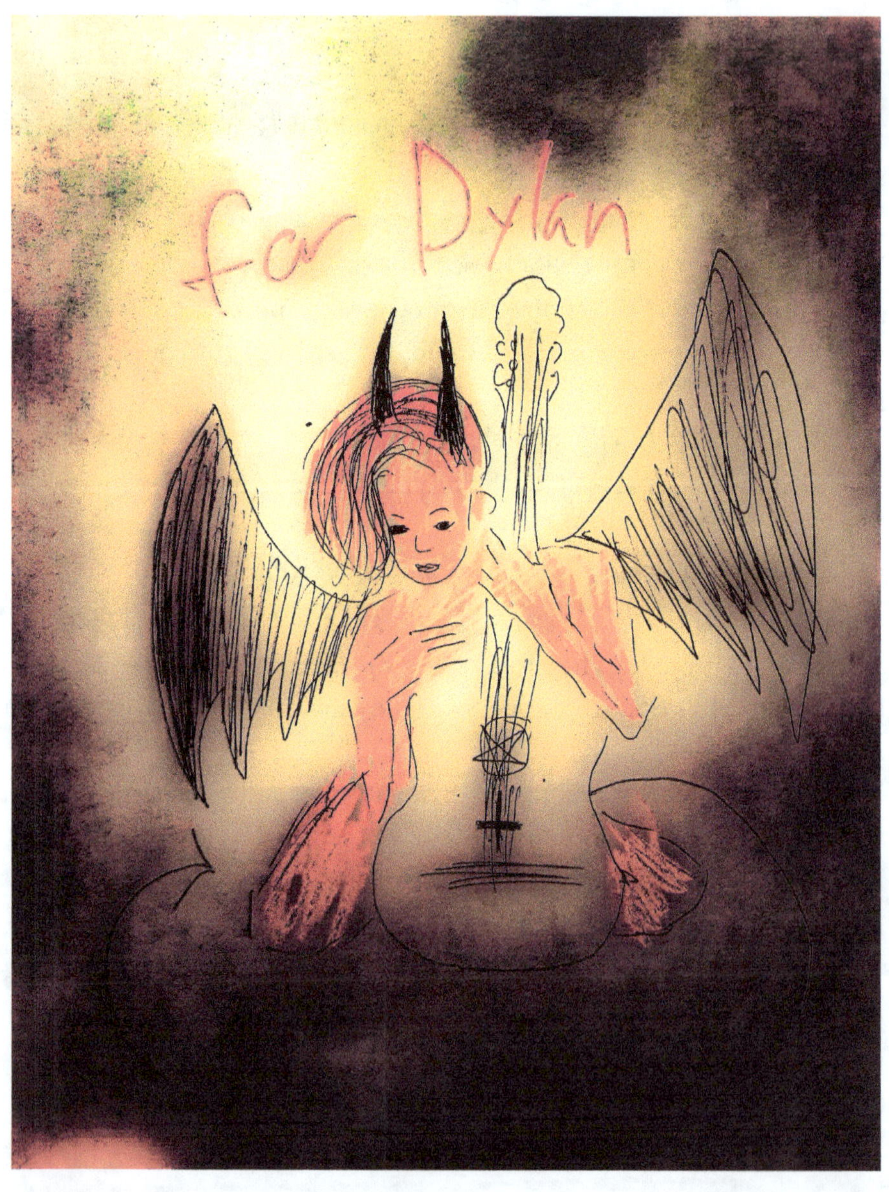

10

My mother hath callen again. Why must the old seek to pester the young?? I am doing verily well, I say so myself, but all she does is try to keep giving me money!!

I told her that she must use that money to buy shares in apples!! For humanity's one most vile sin is the one with us eating the apple! If we keep buying shares in apples, we'll eventually have enough to get rid of pride!

She sayeth, "I don't know... Are you sure you don't need to come home? You seem like you're in a difficult spot... Your dad said you still have that infestation of fleas in your apartment as well..."

I sayeth on the phone, "No! I am doing God's will here! I am reaching my true calling and potential!!"

"...I understand that you think you're doing the right thing, but I just don't want you to get locked up again-" she sayeth.

"What foolishness... That was a complete misunderstanding, you know this! I got out without a sin on my name! It was just Babylon trying to waste my time!" I said.

"...I know. Just- Call us if you ever need anything, ok?" she said.

"Goodbye, Mother. I must continue my holy duty. The Devil's Daughter walks amongst us." I said.

"What?? But-" she sayeth, but I have hung up by now.

I drew the Devil's Daughter in my flea ridden apartment, wary of the hidden rats who snicker at me and eat my cheese.

I draw her for you, Ma. May the old rest easily. I am A ok.

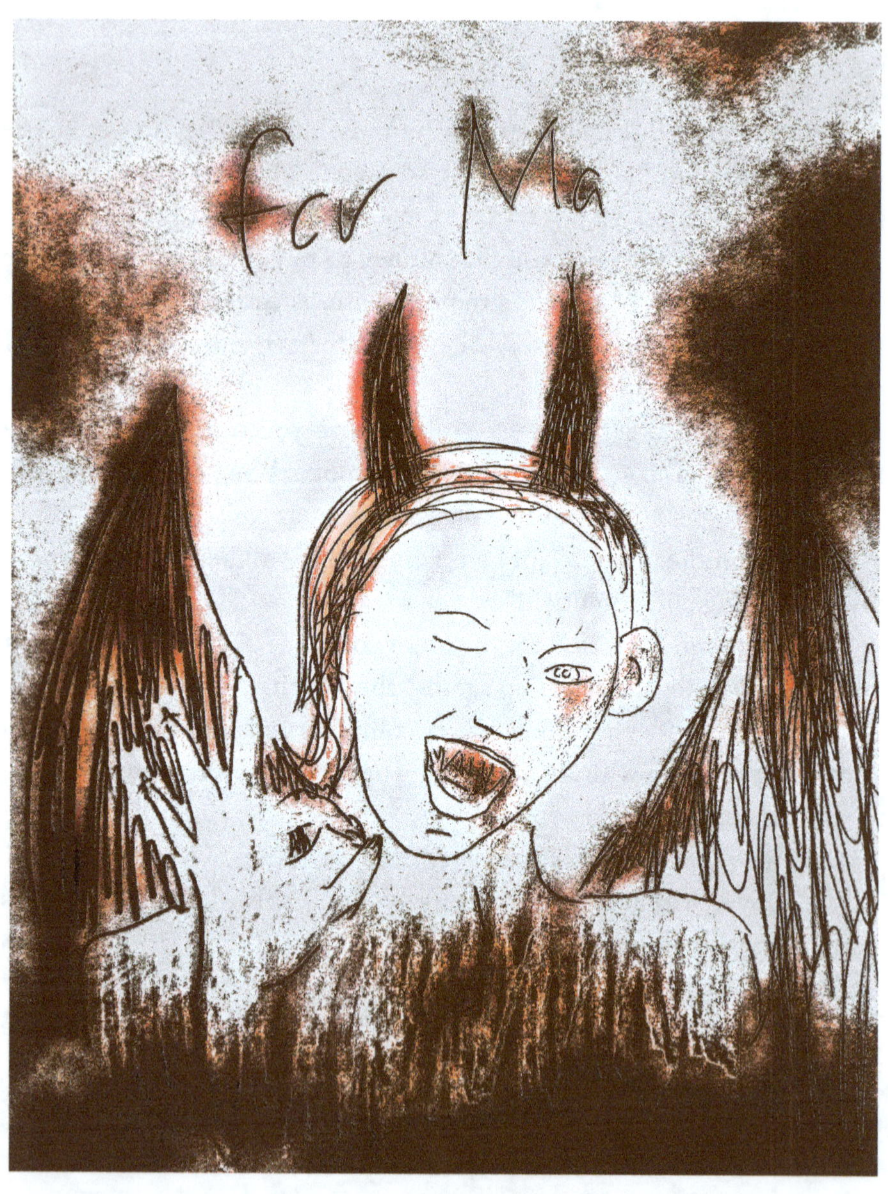
Fcr Ma

11

I have cometh home from another glorious day of fulfilling God's work, and what do I see on the sofa? The she beast, the Daughter of the Devil herself.

She smiled, and said, *"You live in a pretty righteous pad. Sorry, but I wanted to check up on you and your door was unlocked."*

"You break into my home, like many a hidden rat, and come to steal my cheese soul. You are villainous, and you must leave immediately." I said, arms crossed.

"Sorry. I won't intrude again... Rats?" she said.

"Look! Look there. Under the fridge is a hole!" I said, pointing at the fridge.

She bent low before me, and I tried to avert my gaze.

She said, *"That's really bad, man. Have you told the landlord?"*

"He doeseth not care. He's trying to get me out of my home, so does nothing at all to fix up the property. He would evict me, but we signed a contract, close to one with the Devil... But God is truly upon my side!" I said.

"...I can help fix it. I'll come back with traps, poison, some flea powder too-" she said.

I was about to refuse, but I felt so tired from all the pests in my place, in my mind, in the world.

I sayeth, "If you allow me to do so righteously with you."

She looked back at me, smiled, and said, *"Ok! This is gonna be so much fun! Big fat rat traps, the military kind! I'll see ya!"*

And with an awful snap, each rat was disemboweled by her traps. The flea powder stank like poison, too.

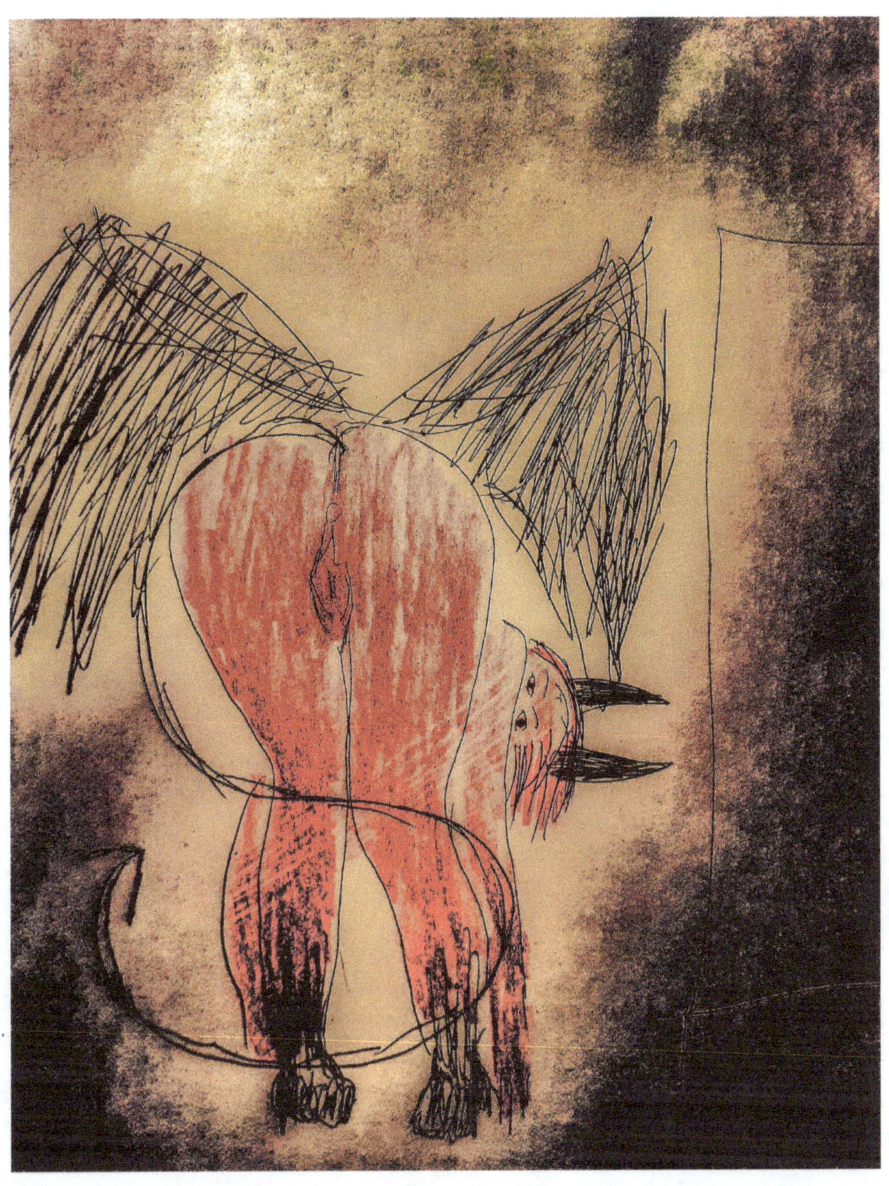

12

After we had ripped every poor rat to shreds, she said, *"...I see you like drawing. Drawing me, especially."* looking at my pictures.

"They are one of those pictures cops draw to find the suspect. It is law, that I am partaking in, and not degeneracy." I said.

"...I can get that. Not that I mind. I think it's kinda cool. Want me to pose for you??" she said, almost desperately.

"...I suppose it would be nice to capture you live, rather than in my fevered mind's eye..." I said, "So that I may show your true evil to all the world."

She laughed, and said, *"Cool. I really like that, actually. Here, lemme lay on the sofa..."*

I quickly said, knowing she wanted to tempt me with some ludicrously filthy pose, that I will draw her at the table.

"...On the table?" she said.

"On the chair. I wish to look into your eyes." I said.

She smiled, and said, *"That's so sweet! Cool."*

I stared into her eyes, as she smiled politely.

"You don't mind if I smoke, do you?" she asked. I shook my head and she started a cigarette.

I drew her as the light from the moon illumined her features... in the shadows of my apartment in a late night... and bahgod, I think I saw something... dare I say... human in her.

I gasped, and drew as much as I could, shading out her hellish features.

I said I was finished, and she got up and looked over my shoulder.

She said, *"I look nice. Like I really belong here! Can I keep this?"*

I shrugged. I would prefer not to have something that showed evil in a goodly light of the moon...

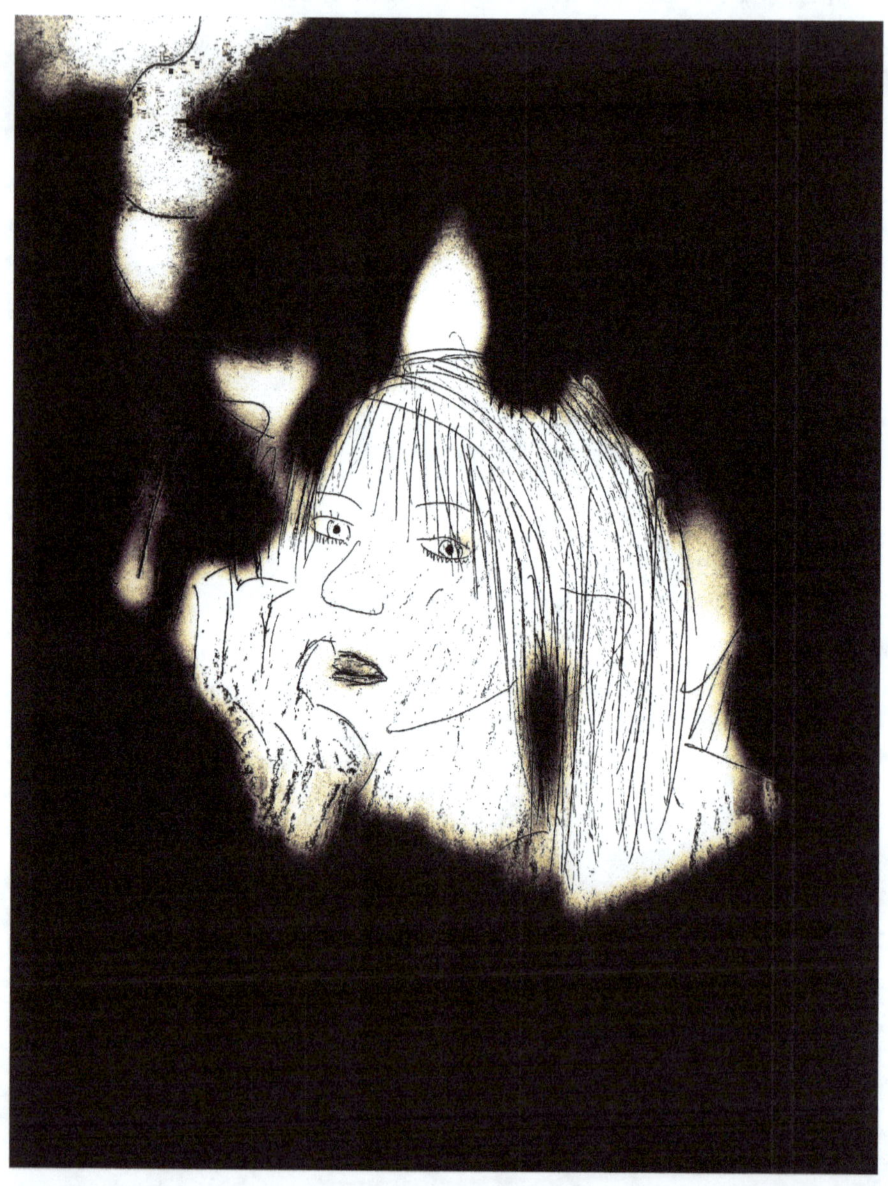

13

The Devil's Daughter tried to set me up with someone.

I stared stonily into this woman's eyes, knowing she was some trick of the she beast.

The woman was nice, albeit hardly clothed, had funny jokes which I didn't dare laugh at in case she might strike after I am exposed, and tried to take me home.

I declined, and said, "You sow. You needn't try to trap me to make love. The Lord watches you, especially you, in times of crisis. Go now, and pray, lest you be damned."

The woman then ran away, crying in the street.

"Why did you say that?! She's just getting over an abusive relationship, and really just needed someone to treat her nice!!" the Devil's Daughter said to me.

"I do not trust you, especially *you*. You and her are probably in cahoots, and trying to steal my soul like my wallet." I said.

"I don't need your money, man. I just needed her to be happy... She was contemplating suicide when I found her, just staring off the bridge like that..." the she beast said.

"I doubt that. Probably was just contemplating a swim, and you expected the worst and decided to seduce her to evil." I said.

"...From forty feet off the ground? You're one heartless bastard, man... Call me when you get a hold of that attitude." she said, shaking her head and walking away.

Call her?

Why would I have her number?

I looked at my phone, and she sent me a Devil smiley face.

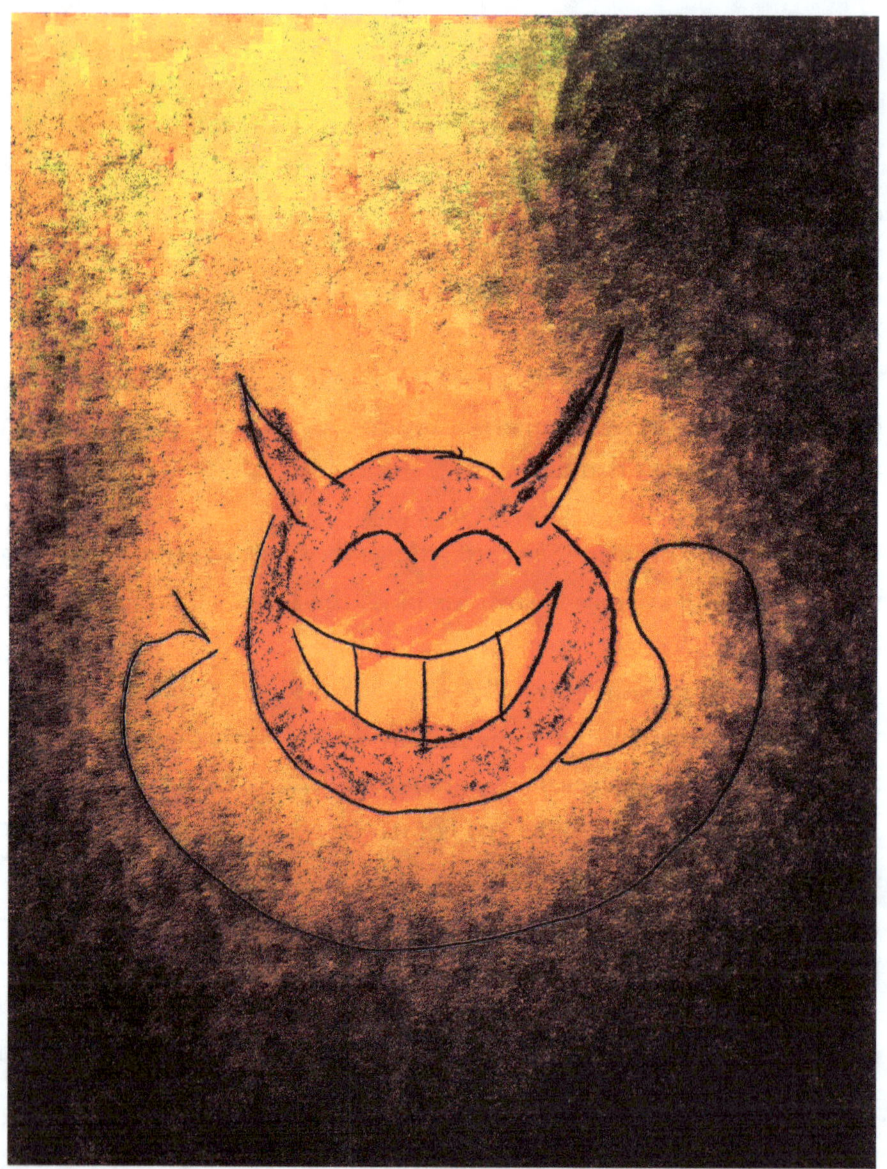

14

I drew her as I sat beside her as she drank beer by the harbor. Evil... heartless... she beast...

"You seem nice, but I think you're a bit crazy." she said to me.

I continued drawing, ignoring her wretched comment, and she sighed, and continued to drink her beer.

"Like, why are you even obsessed with me? I just thought you were cute. I'd say you're my first friend I made here, but you really don't seem like you have the capacity for friends." she said.

I laughed sharply at her sinister comment, and continued to draw.

"...You mean you actually have people other than your family you can talk to?" she said

I snorted, and drew.

"I get that life is tough, but you gotta try making it nicer for some people. They have it even worse." she said.

I sighed, and continued drawing as she drank her beer.

"I know, right?? People are all stuck on something, then on another, and all we do is ignore it and prefer to live our own lives. It was so much easier in Hell, where people are bad because they're bad. Here, it's not so simple." she said.

I stared hard into her eyes, and she blinked. I continued to draw.

She kissed me, and I thought I would scream.

She ran away giggling, as I tried to wipe the feeling of the Devil's Daughter off my lips.

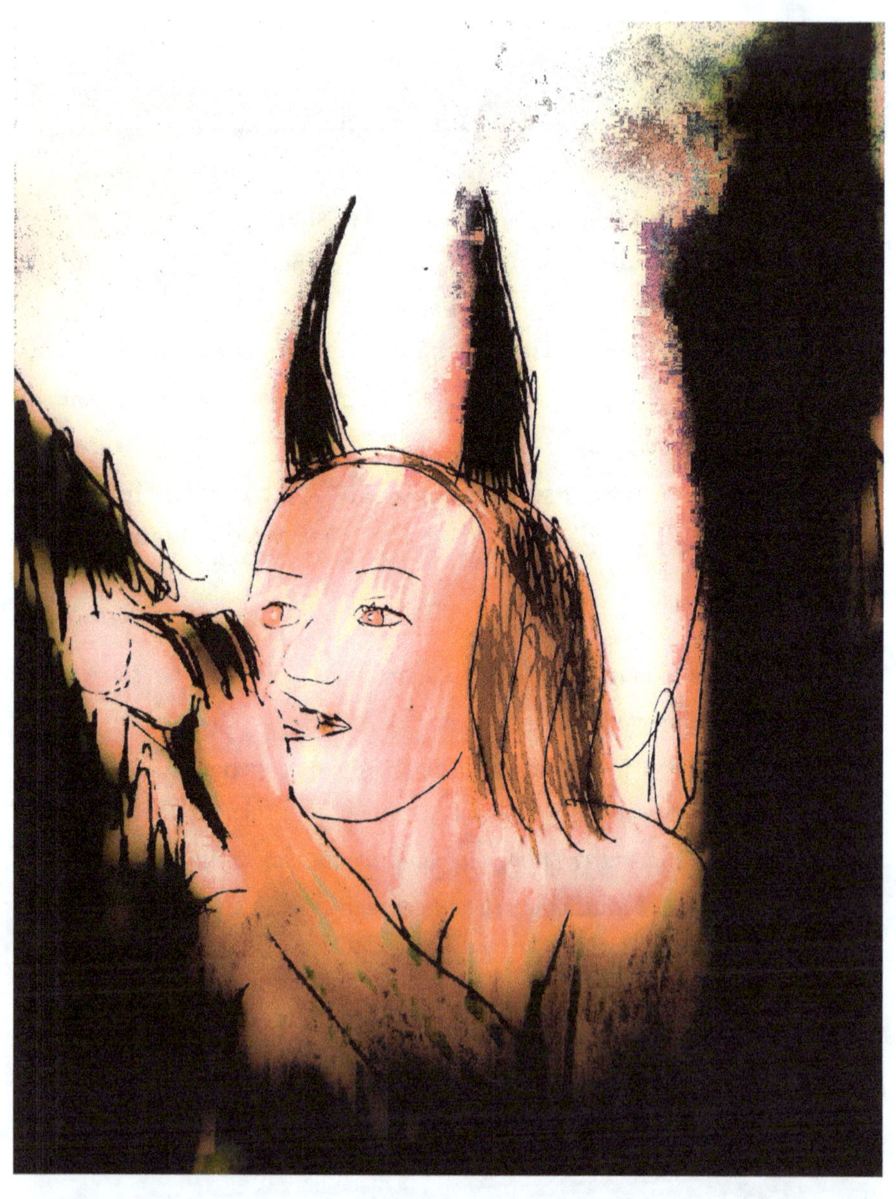

15

"So... I see you found a girl? Finally?" my dad said, looking at my drawings as he had invited himself over to my apartment.

"None of your business... I mean, it is all of everyone's business that the Devil's Daughter has invaded creation and seeks to force her will on the-" I said.

My dad laughed, cutting me off, and said, "Yeah, women are all like that. Try to give her some crappy token of affection, like flowers or something. It's weird how chicks even like that crap... I mean, for a guy, give me a beer and a kiss, and I'll forgive her for anything."

"...I see. Will that drive her off, as well?" I said.

My dad opened his eyes wide, and said, "...You're kidding. You mean she actually *likes* you? Well, I suppose that's good, although she might be the crazy sort... Oh well, enjoy it while it lasts. I see you got rid of the fleas! I feel you got rid of the fleas, because they're not jumping on me..."

"The Devil's Daughter and I expunged them from my sanctuary. It was tough, and we had to air out the whole bed-" I said.

"Good. If anything, keep cleanly. Women appreciate that the most. She's a right good looker, isn't she! I mean... you got her to pose nude and everything for you! She must really dig you. I can't wait to have grandkids... Don't mess it up! Do you need anything? I only came over because your ma *insisted...*" he said.

"No. I just need-" I said.

My dad was starting to cry, and I asked why.

"You're finally self sufficient. I'm so happy." he said, and hugged me.

The Devil's Daughter was smirking at me, sitting on my windowsill. For Dad, may you see the true evil one day.

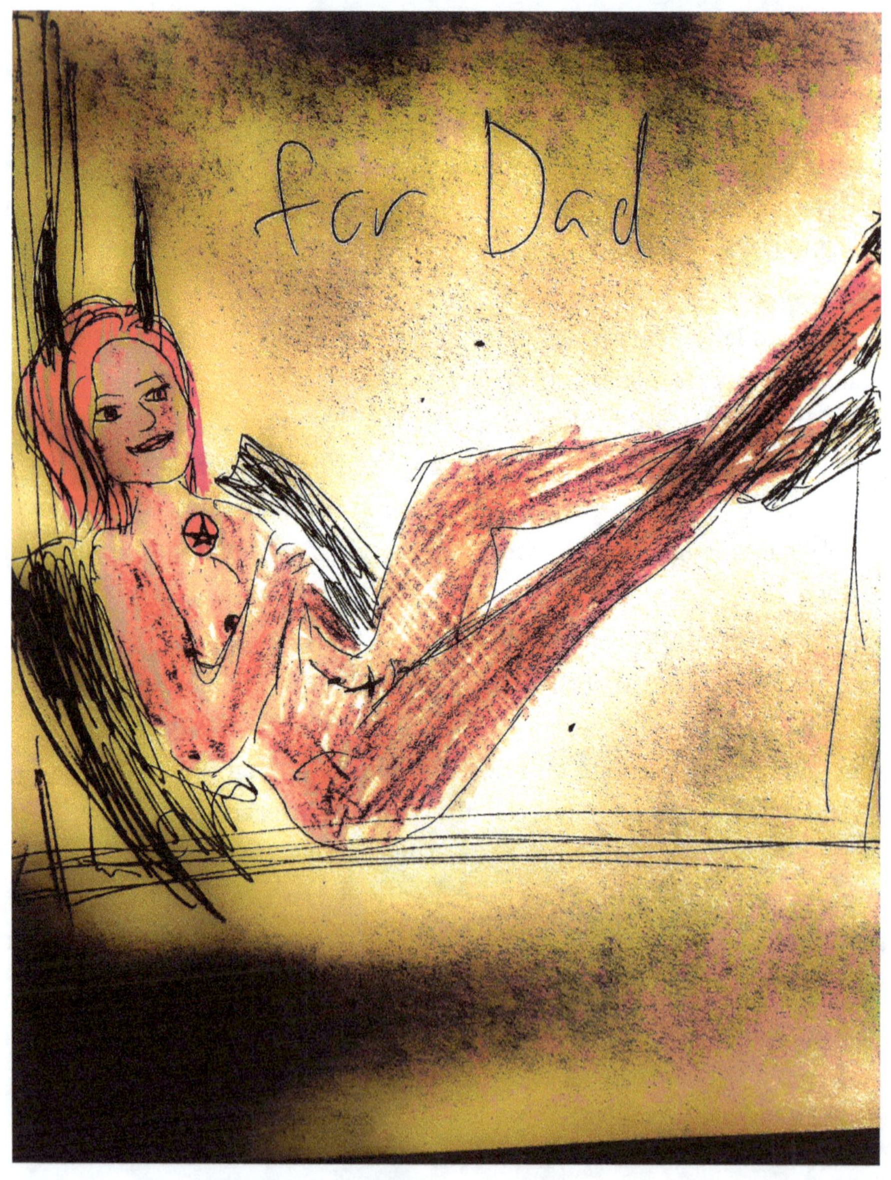

16

"Hmm… I really don't see anything great in these." the art gallery owner said.

"But it is a slice of life! It is real evil, a hellish form-" I said.

"These are all fantasies of some demon chick. It's not realistic, and not what we want to portray. If anything, it is base smut with silly wings and horns. And why is her skin red?" he asked.

"She's the Daughter of the Devil! Obviously she has red skin." I said.

"…Ok. You keep up with that, and don't give up! Maybe take an art class or two?" he said, with that phony smile.

"…We'll keep in touch?" I said.

"We'll call you. Good day." he said, and left my home.

I slammed the door, as he had forgotten to shut it.

I furiously… felt very deelevated. I was doing God's work, sending in every little bit of real news to the newspaper… but nothing got published. The Devil's Daughter is amongst us!! Why did no one care but me?

I wanted to write another stirring, fantastic piece on the grey morality of the world, I wanted to show the world the true evil stalking creation… but I don't know.

I guess I felt I would never be fulfilled.

I didn't feel like crying. I didn't feel like anything mattered, and every tear would be a waste of salt water.

The Devil's Daughter came out of the bathroom, and said, *"Is he gone? Let's do the one of me eating a peach."*

I sighed, and drew the Devil's Daughter eating a peach.

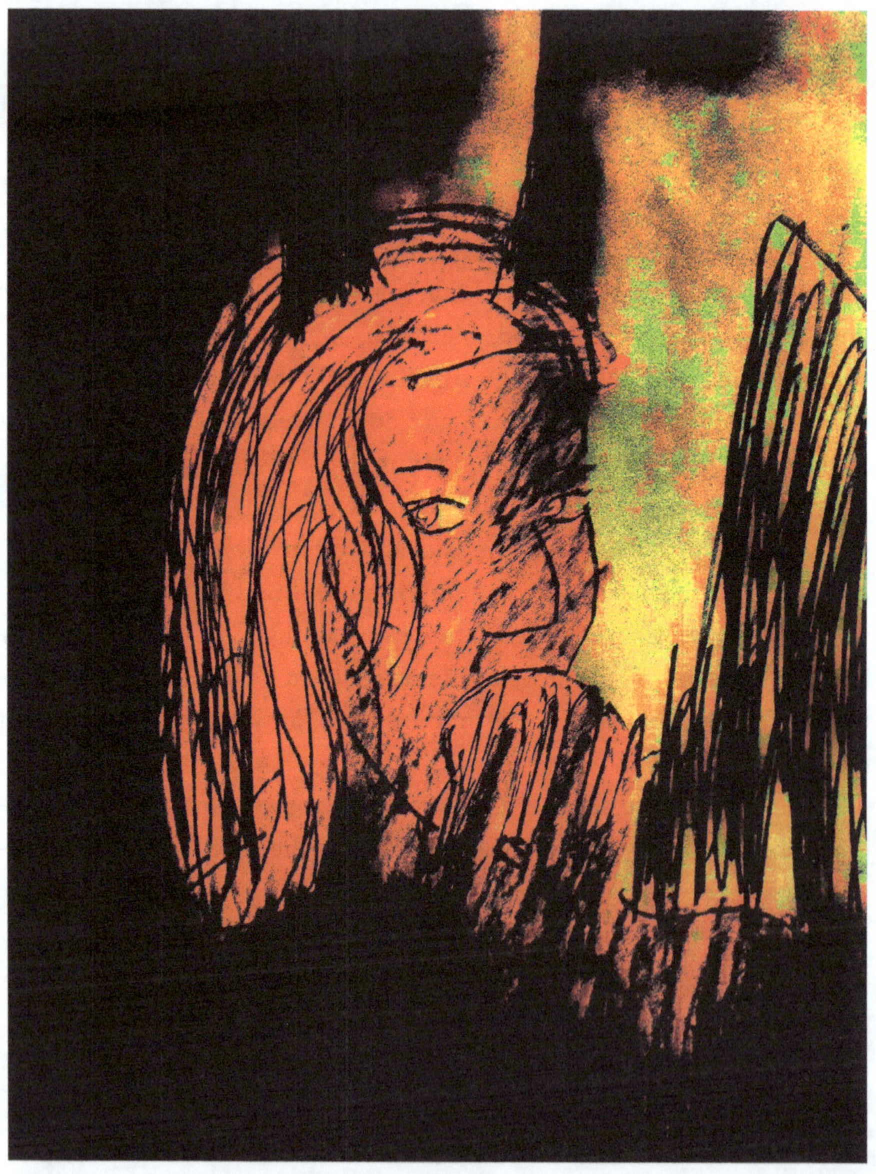

17

"*...So this is your muse?*" the Devil asked his daughter in a dream.

"*Well, I'm more his muse. You know I just can't get over how nice life is, but he does inspire me sometimes on the guitar.*" the Devil's Daughter said.

The Devil said, "*...Why an actually crazy guy? Don't you think you should be tempting a priest?*"

"*This guy could be a priest though! He's so stirring when he speaks, and is so enlightened! Have you seen his art of me?*" she said.

"*...I think you're seeing things through tinted shades. This guy wouldn't even belong in Hell, because he's so worthless. How about you-*" the Devil said.

"*Quit telling me what to do, Dad!! I can make my own choices, and if I want to seduce a nice, normal, crazy person, then that's my choice!!*" she said.

I quickly realized I was in the picture, and began praying.

I began drawing the picture, in a dream.

When I woke up, I was passed out with my head on my table, with the empty bottle of booze beside me.

I have sinned. All I must do is ask for forgiveness. I *must.*

The Devil's Daughter was sleeping on my couch. What lies. She knows she was in my dreams just now.

She winked an eye open at me, and tried to feign sleeping again, rolling over.

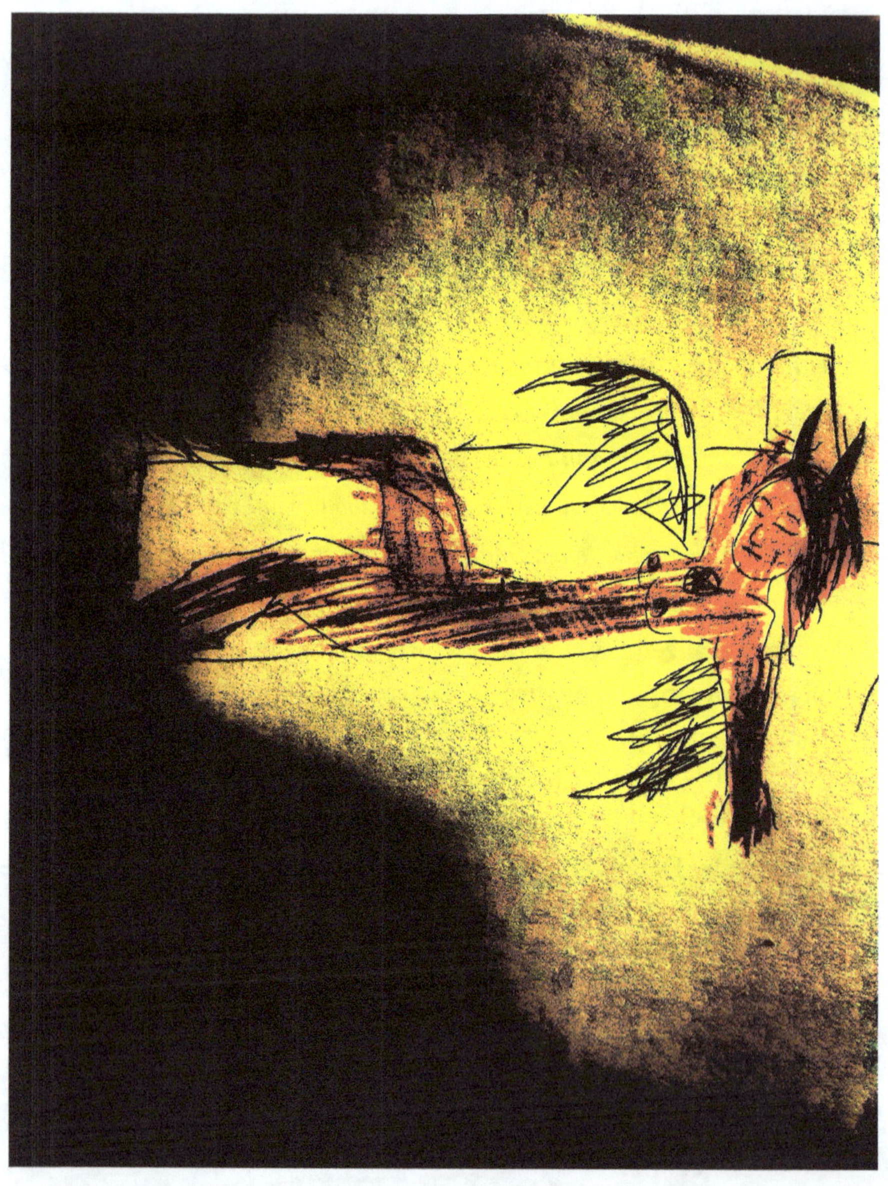

18

"Are you embarrassed of your feet?" I asked the Devil's Daughter as she... *she* treated me for pancakes for breakfast.

"Um... No! Why? Should I be?" she said, putting her feet further under the table.

"I mean, maybe, yes, they are goat's hooves. There is nothing so unappealing to normal, righteous people. Maybe some perverts find that attractive, but I think it is inhuman." I said.

She stared down at her pancakes, and ate a bite. *"Good food, eh?"* she said.

I felt saddened, as she tried to hide her feet more under the table.

"I am... I am woeful of your condition. I don't know what it's like to be half monster. Your hooves do make my art look a little more surreal, however, and show that... animalistic ferocity, yeah, of evil." I said.

She smiled, and said, *"What makes you think I'm not full monster?"*

I said, "...Didn't the Devil seduce some poor young virgin, corrupting her so that she'd fall to Hell, probably rape her, and have her give birth to you?"

The Devil's Daughter laughed, and said, *"My dad said my mama was a nasty young thing, with a heart of gold. Pyrite, false gold, really. She took even the Devil for a loop, to get his hoards of... well, all he's really got is Hell, which is all wasteland. When my mother knew this, she ditched me on the Devil's doorstep, and I never met her."*

"...I'm sorry. That must've been tough." I said.

"Not really. My dad's a good guy, to me, anyway. I'd say there's lots of nasty things you can say about your partner's parents, though, so keep that in mind when I have to bring yours up..." she said.

I gulped, and nearly choked on my pancake.

Partner?

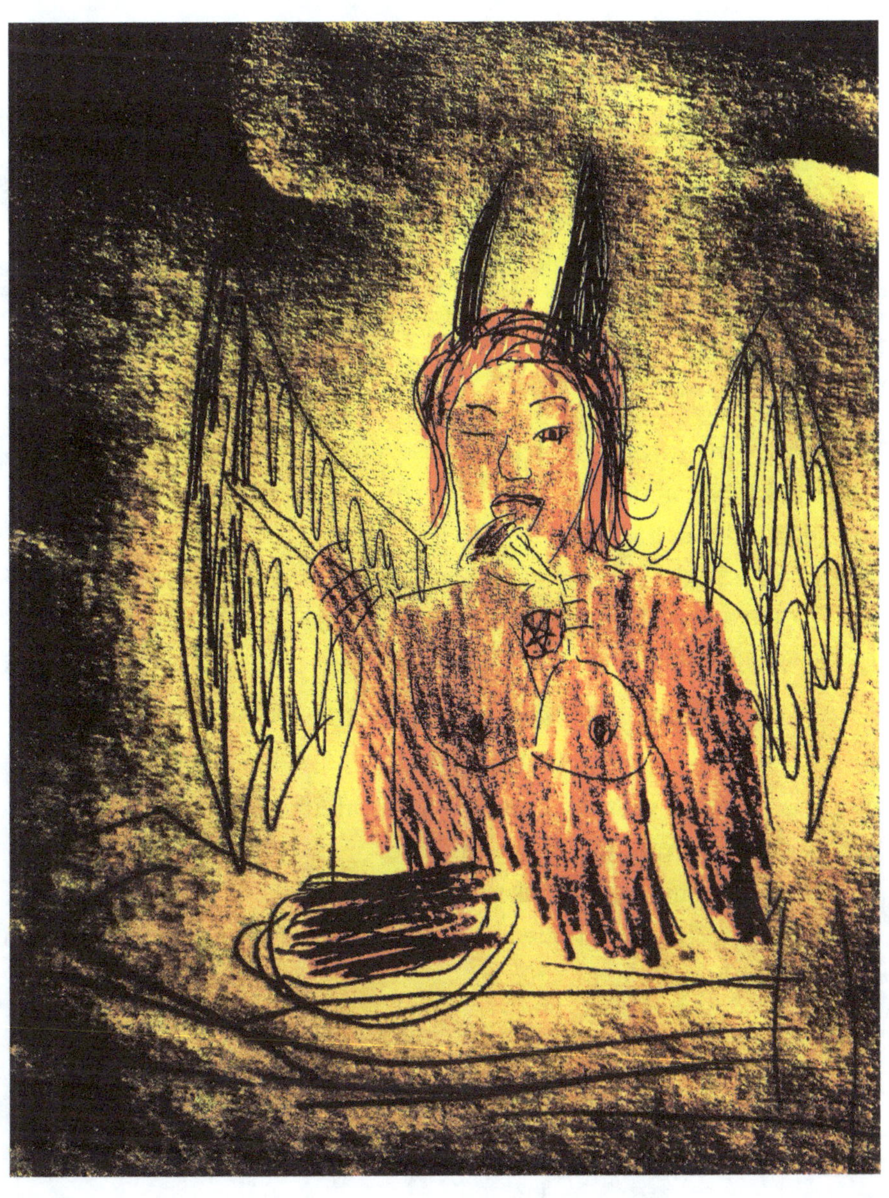

19

The Devil's Daughter followed me home, and she said, *"I was aborted."*

"...Oh. So that is what you meant about being left on the Devil's doorstep, as the unbaptized, aborted fetuses go to Hell-" I said.

"No. The Devil was just the only one who really wanted me. God would've taken me if the Devil wasn't so vehemently my claimant. I sometimes wonder what it would've been like to be brought up by God himself..." the Devil's Daughter said.

I cleared my throat, and tried to lose her at my doorstep.

"Well! It was a nice breakfast. Let's do it again sometime- I mean, begone, blasted fiend!!" I said.

She stared hard into my eyes. She just stared into my eyes.

"...What are you doing? Trying to hypnotize me?" I said.

She shrugged, and said, *"Thought it'd turn you on, looking into my eyes. They really are a very erotic part of the body, now that you've mentioned it to me. It's like... looking into someone's soul."*

I was going to shut my eyes, so she wouldn't try and steal my soul... but she smiled at me, and my heart froze.

I drew her smiling as I was safe in my apartment alone, and the feeling it invoked in me terrified me. Not least because of the fangs, but also... something I couldn't place.

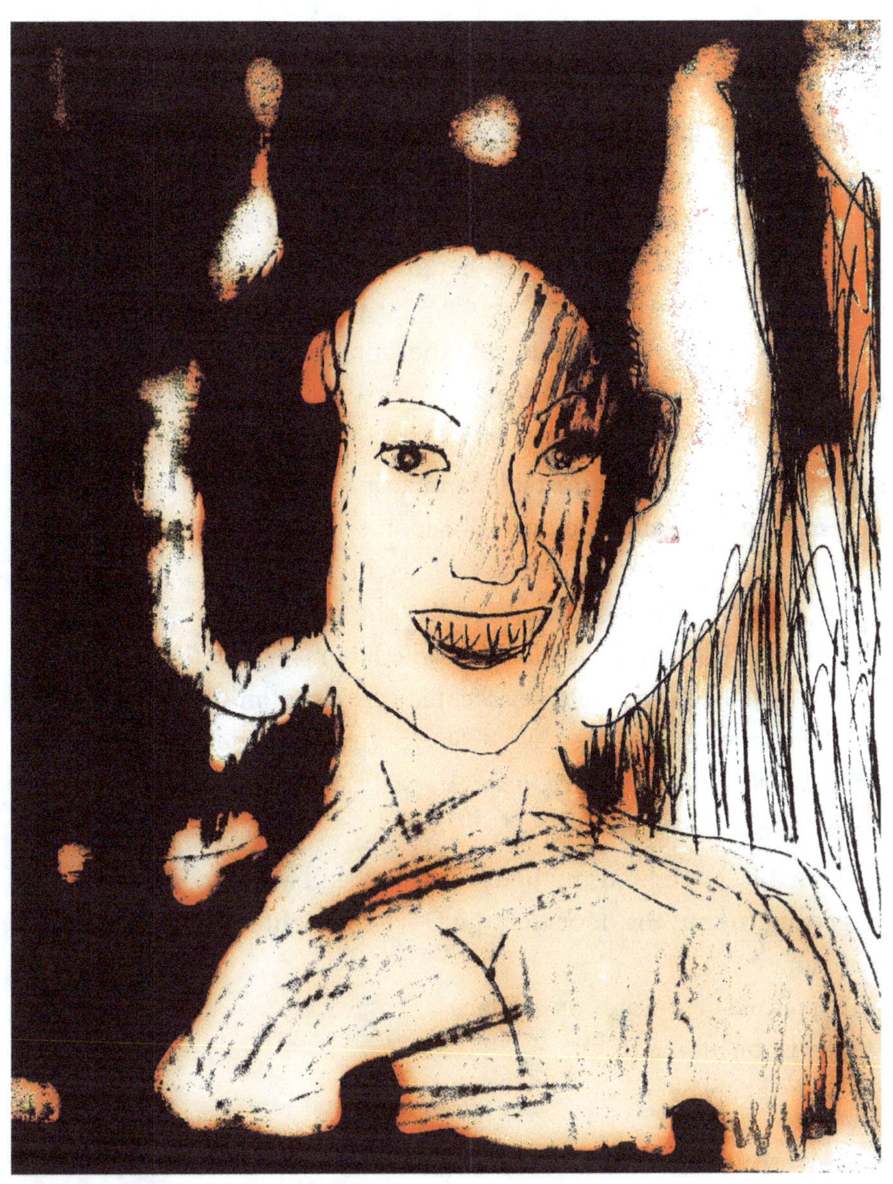

20

I did not realize that evil was flirting with *me...* Shouldn't it be the other way around??

I needed to remain hidden. I needed to exorcise this woman- this vile fiend from my life. I could not let her grasp at my soul, as she was already grasping at my heart...

BAHGOD. She's knocking on the door. I quickly jumped on the couch and pretended to be asleep.

"Are you there? Do you even go anywhere? C'mon... Open up! It's me!" she said, in that guise of comfortable familiarity.

I strangely... wanted to open the door.

I strangely... wanted to look at her again.

I strangely... wanted to kiss her, like she had to me.

I nearly did when I had already done the first two of these things.

It looked like she would've accepted this kiss of mine.

She blinked an eye open, as she was preparing herself for the kiss, and said, *"Woah. You look fucked, man. Are you having a stroke? Half your body looks like it's trembling."*

I tried to straighten my body, and walked back into the apartment, forgetting to shut the door that the Devil's Daughter walked in after me through.

I splashed cold water on my face.

I must be insane.

I must truly be nuts.

For I was just about to throw my soul away for a kiss.

I asked her, "Am I really a madman?"

She tried to look around the room, looked at her feet, looked up at me, and said, *"Do you want to talk about it?"*

I sat at the sofa, and sighed as she sat next to me and listened to my woes and betoils.

"I was called mad by the courts. They let me out on insanity. It was a completely overblown situation… And the only reason I was jailed while the court was mulling over my position was because the cops made cases against me… and not my dad who I got in a fight with." I said.

"You fought with your father?" she asked.

"I was mad! I was going insane because… because of this hallucinogenic drug. It made me nuts! I don't feel right telling you this… I feel like you may use it against me…" I said.

"It's alright, you don't have to talk about if you don't-"

"It was Hell, in that jail cell. It was Hell trying to straighten out my mind again. It is Hell now, when I feel the old scars come forth, rupture, into… well, you. I know you must be some evil trick-" I said.

She shrugged, and said, *"My friends think I'm real."*

"…Then am I mad for thinking you're not?" I said.

She held my hand. She squeezed it. I accepted it.

I burst down crying, and she hugged me.

"Wanna do something to take your mind off that whole thing?" she said.

I said, "I- I want to draw. It is soothing to me."

"Cool. I'll pose nice! I love how you picture my eyes so perfectly! Can you… Can you draw my legs? With my… my hooves?" she said, almost desperately.

I smiled, wiped off the tears, straightened up, and told her to be professional, and I will draw her well.

She sat on the sofa edge.

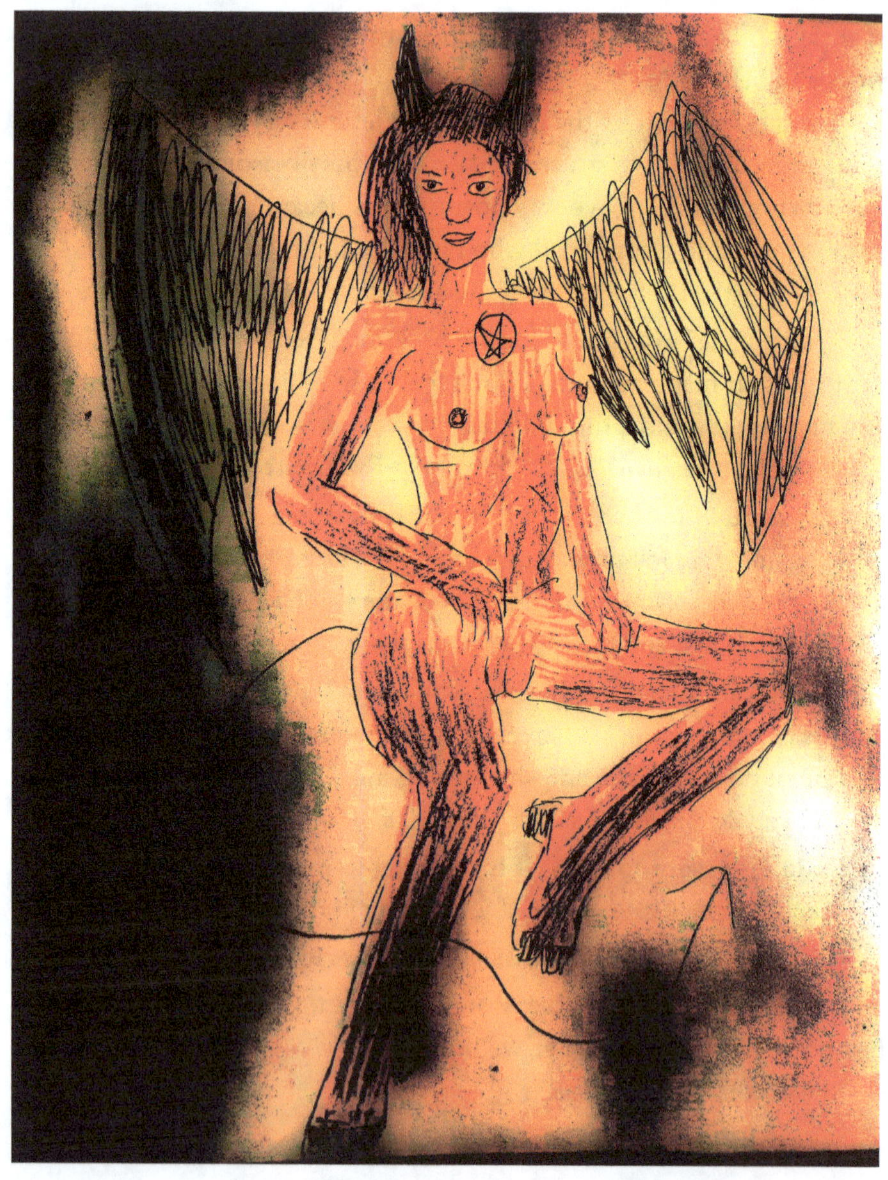

21

I said to her, "What if I am Jesus Christ, come down incognito, even to myself?"

She said, *"Isn't everyone Jesus? Like, Jesus is in all of us, or something."*

I said, "But I will never be everyone else! So how can I know what *anyone* really is?"

She said, *"How can you be Jesus if you can't be everyone?"*

"...What if this is a dream?" I said.

She said, *"I'd get naked and run around, if this was a dream. Oh wait, I'm already doing that..."* and smirked.

I laughed, and said, "I don't think we ever have gotten introduced properly. My name's-"

She put a finger to my lips, and said, *"I don't want to know your name, man. I just want you to be happy while you can. We don't need to dilute our relationship with feelings or petty things like names. We attach too much to our significance, when you're simply an artist, and I am your muse. Let's keep it simple."*

"...Ok, my muse." I said.

She grinned, and said, *"Now, I like that. It sounds... Hot! How come you've never flirted with me before??"*

I blushed, and said, "You're a vile she beast who has come to take creation. How can I flirt with someone I know wants to kill and eat my soul?"

She said, *"You make the most of it. We may meet later if I ever desire to go back home again and you die of some stupid artist death... Like suicide. I hate that route of death..."*

"I have thought about it, before. It is very tempting, when you believe you'll never make anything out of your life anyway." I said.

She sighed, and said, *"Why don't all the old bastards who've had their fill of life kill themselves? It doesn't make sense that the young want to die."*

"...I suppose. It is a very evil way of coming to terms with life, that you should be dead." I said.

"Exactly my thoughts. Ready for another?" she said.

"All yours, muse." I said, and I drew the next pose.

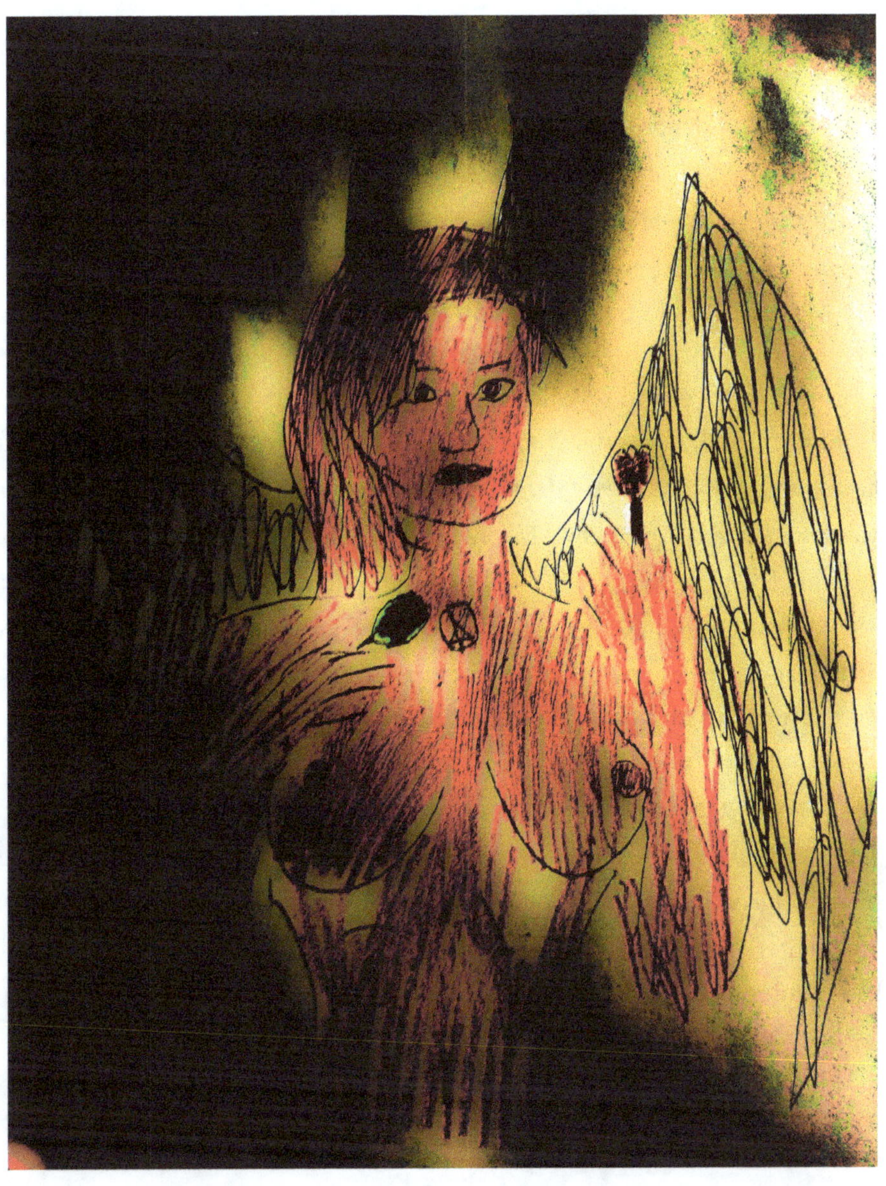

22

"I was going to practice at leading you to the bed to try and take your man-hood, but I feel silly at that plot. My dad wants me to be so good at trying to take mortals' decency, and all that... Sometimes I just get sick of it." she said, as we were sitting on the couch.

"Maybe I should try to take you to the bed? Seduce the seducer? Does that really count though, if we're keeping score? We both would end up just making love, and no one would get any points." I said.

She giggled, and said, *"I think that's the way it should be. If people don't keep score. You can't have a decent relationship if every little thing is held over your head like a big baseball bat, ready to smack your partner down if they don't hold a bigger bat."*

"My dad loves baseball. All he ever talks about. Tried getting me into little league teams and all sorts of crap... I was stuck in outfield, throwing the mitt up and down to myself, like a fool..." I said.

"In a game??" she said.

"Especially in a game. I got bored out there." I said.

She laughed, and said, *"And now you're a hotshot artist. You must've sold scores of pictures already. Why aren't you revered like the old masters yet?"*

"Quit flattering, vile she beast- muse. I am not really that good... Everyone says so." I said, looking at my feet.

She said, *"Beauty is in the eye of the beholder. Do you find me beautiful?"*

I looked back at her, and the yes in my throat was stuck.

"*You doing that seizure thing again? Let me pose something nice.*" she said, and she posed.

She turned her back to me, and stuck a hand at the table.

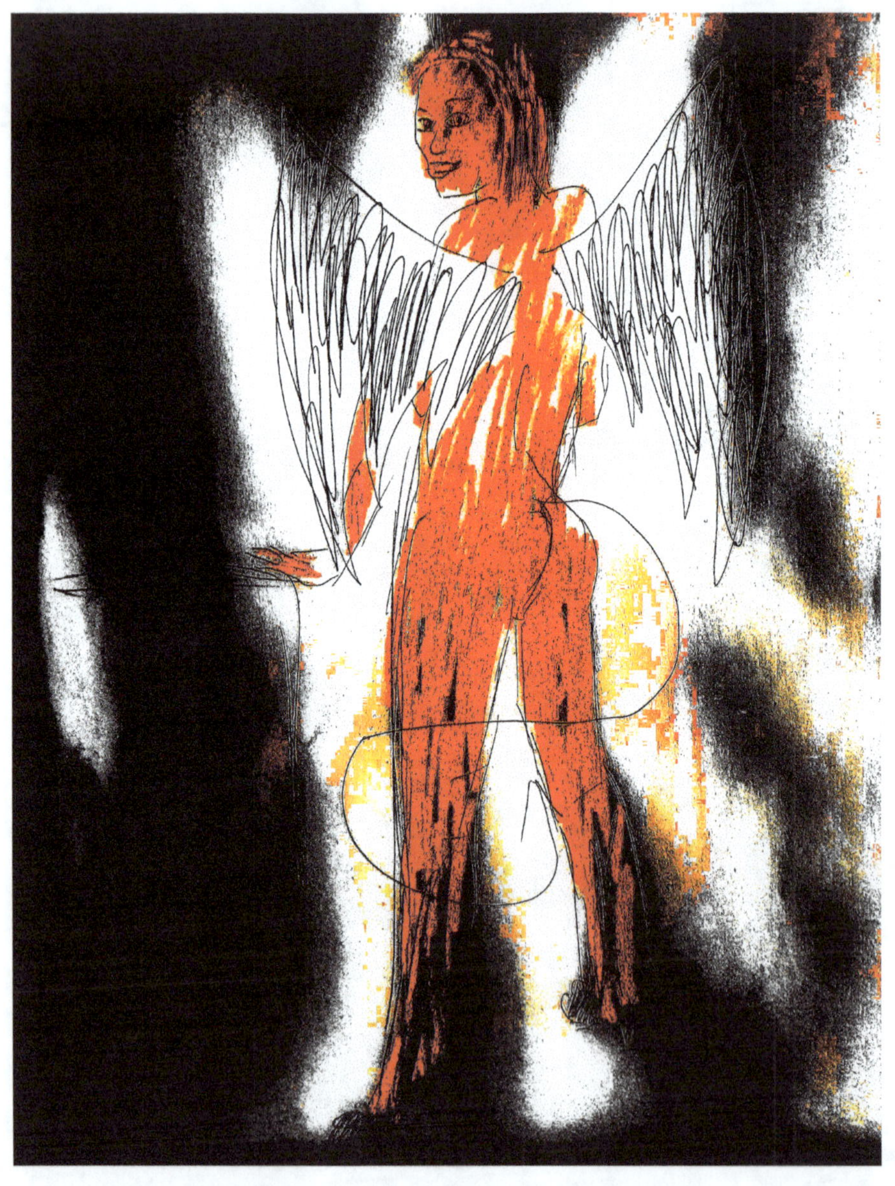

23

"Gosh, my legs look nice. You capture my good sides! Some men think women are only butts and boobs, but legs really make the pic." she said, looking at my picture.

"I think this one could've been nicer… And why do you always point at your vagina with your tail??" I said.

"That's another big pointer. If you didn't like it you wouldn't have drawn it!" she said, laughed, then sighed, "Do you want me to try and seduce you? Now that I've brought it up, it might be fun? I don't know, because now you're expecting something like that…"

"Um… ergm… That was my biggest fear you would try to do to me." I said.

"Oh! Ok. Then I won't-"

"And also my greatest desire. I can admit that. Heck, if I can admit madness, why not admit lust for the Devil's Daughter?" I said.

"I'm glad you purposed that phrase as 'lust.' It wouldn't have been love, what we would do. It would be just trying to fulfill an urge." she said, rubbing a thigh.

"I… I think I just need some time to think. Maybe pray? I am looking for guidance. Why did you say we were partners?" I asked.

"Sexual partners, maybe? Well, you need a muse for art, and heck, I'ma be your partner if I'ma pose. We're gonna take the world, with these beautiful, gorgeous pics." she said.

"...Ok. I'm hoping God will guide me, in this matter-" I said.

"See ya at church next Sunday?" she said

"...What?" I said.

"Well, a nun is a friend of mine, and I thought it might be a good experience. She used to be quite a party gal, and doesn't judge people like me." she said.

"Do you- Do you sleep with a lot of-" I said.

"Jealous?? Now that's righteous! I love it. I'm not a slut, but I do enjoy a good time. What is it you envision me doing?" she said.

"...I don't really know anymore." I said.

She patted my leg, and said, *"Well, you can have it anytime you want it. My advice is to not think so hard, and just-"*

So I kissed her.

It was a long kiss indeed.

But she broke off, and said, *"And a start of eternal torment begins. You're mine now, and you're gonna fall in Hell with me.*

"Why? Because I like you.

"So... the first time for us we're gonna remember. Buckle up, buckaroo, because you're in for an experience."

She smiled, and I realized what I had done.

She kissed me on the cheek, as I walked her to the door.

She sent me a devil smiley face.

And a pic to remember her by, that I couldn't help but draw.

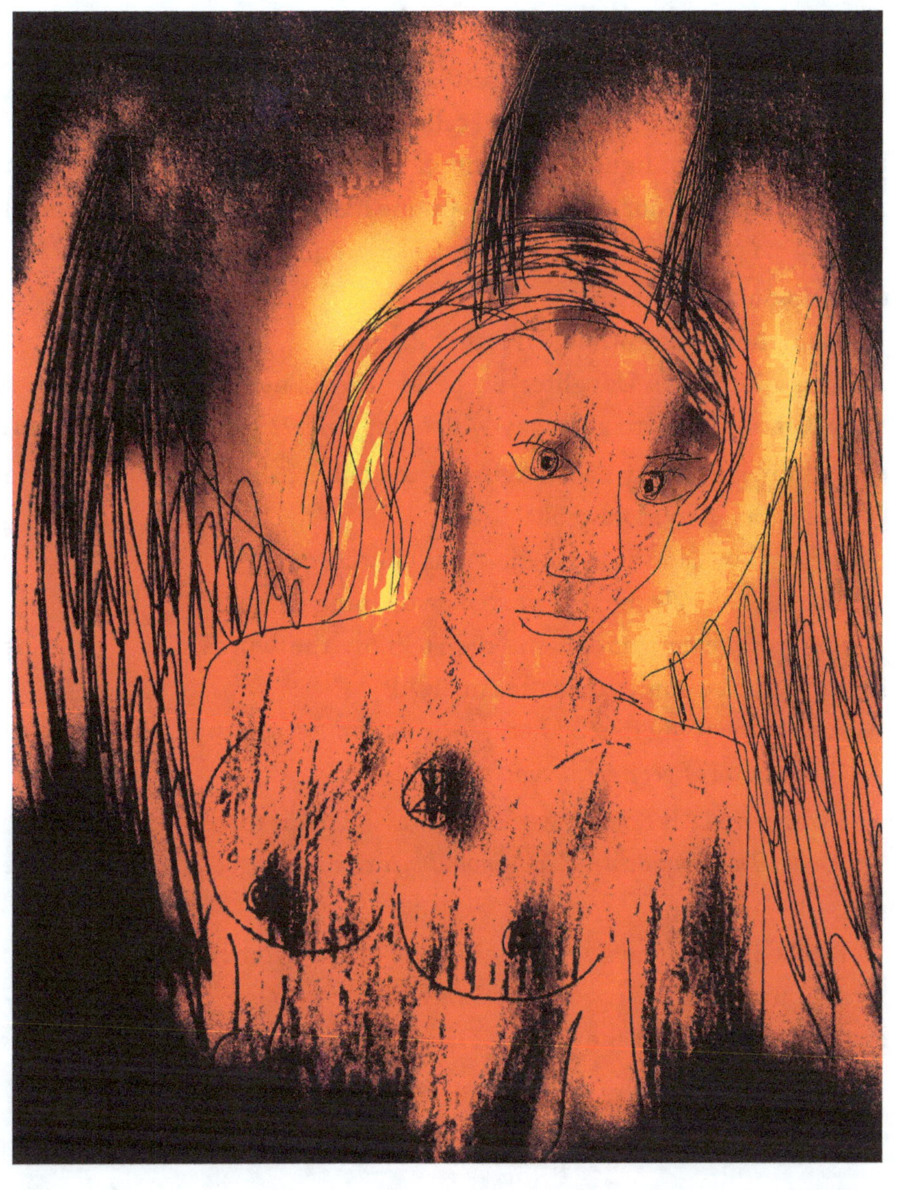

24

The nun was the woman I had called a sow, whom the she beast tried to set me up with. I gulped as I shook the nun's hand, and she stared at me like a viper. "Your words really hit me hard..." she said, "And, when I actually *did* pray, I felt like something was guiding me here. Perhaps you can help out after mass?"

I said there was nothing I'd rather do more!

The vile Devil's Daughter sat beside me in nudity in the church... How come she gets to get away with being nude?? It's not like I *wouldn't* enjoy showing off my naked figure to the public, albeit probably hard to get accustomed to at first, but-

Wait. How can she even enter this church??

She knelt beside me, as I prayed an opening prayer.

She sang, even though she didn't know the words, like I did. She kinda mumbled something after my lead.

And I was going to stop her, as she got up for communion.

"What? Can't I get a treat, too?" she said.

I whispered, "It doesn't work that way!! That is the Body of Christ-"

"Oooh! That sounds delicious. Should be extra, extra good for me, too!" she said, and got in line.

I sighed, following her humming one of the hymns to communion.

The nun was giving out the Body of Christ, after the priest consecrated the host, and the Devil's Daughter chomped on it, said, *"Tastes good! You guys have good cookies!"* and she left to slurp down the entire goblet of the Blood of Christ.

I muttered, as the nun placed the host in my hand-

And I dropped the Body of Christ.

Everyone was staring at me, as I was mortified.

"You can have another-" the nun started saying.

I quickly picked the Body of Christ back up, shoved it in my mouth and swallowed, and would've ran back to my spot in the pew if I could.

I "hung out" with the Daughter of the Devil and the nun after we had cleaned up after mass. The Daughter of the Devil took the nun's habit and wore it, and asked me to draw her, and I did. The nun laughed at her silliness. I sighed.

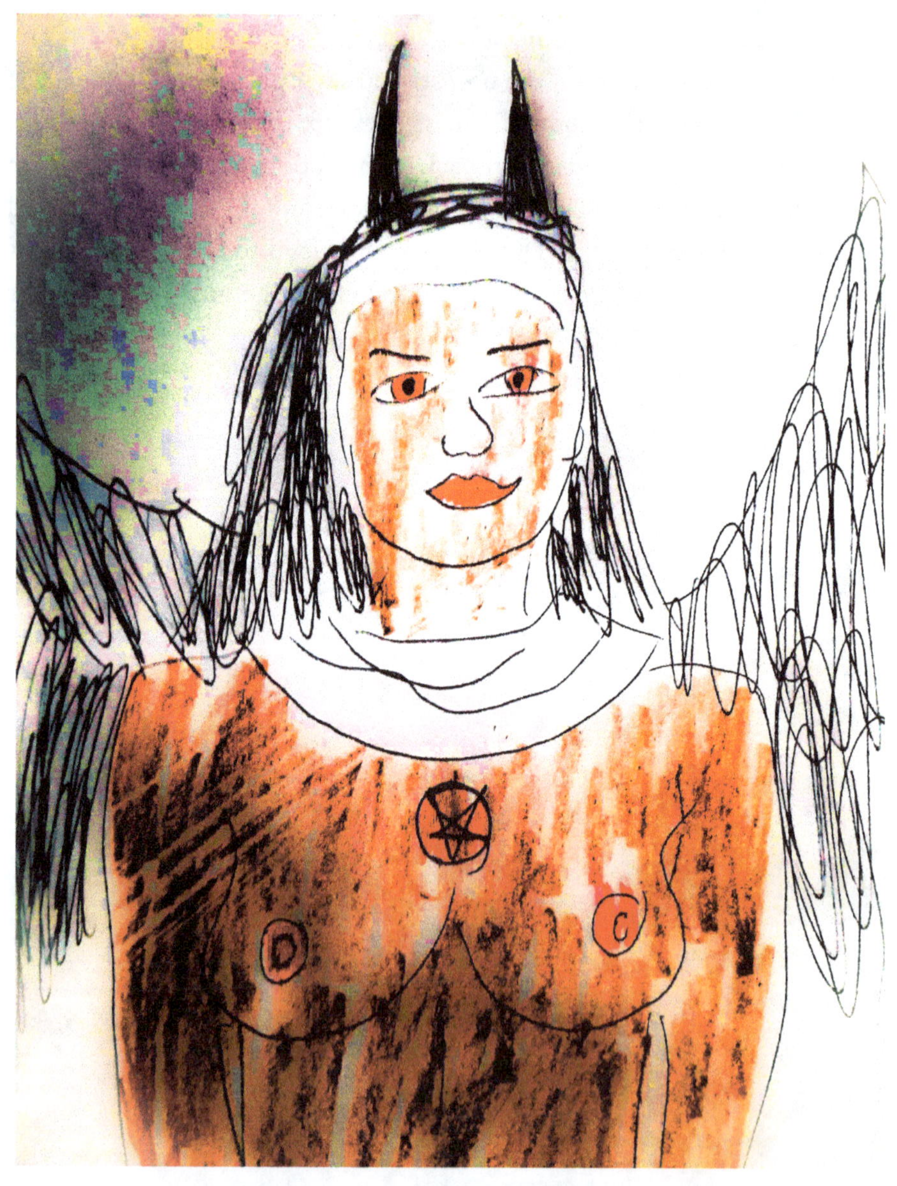

25

I carefully drank only one beer at a bar, and the Devil's Daughter asked me, *"So what's your kinks? I know drawing is a thing for you but-"*

"I do not have 'kinks.' I am as God made me." I said.

"...Crazy? You said yourself that God made you as you are, and you yourself called yourself crazy." she said, slurping at her beer.

I sipped at the beer, and said, "What would I know about kinks?! I do not even know what sort of a thing is!"

"Like the hooves thing. Some people really, really do like that. It's hard to describe why, so it's a kink." she said.

"...Am I catering to perverts, with my art?" I said.

She shrugged, and said, *"Most people look at porn, every once and awhile, are they perverts? Not all of them. Even classical art is considered tasteful, although blatantly showing vagina and penis everywhere you look. Even the Indians made a book about sex positions, and that's classic literature. You have to ask yourself what 'is' perversion?"*

"Deviation from the norm?" I said.

"Exactly. If everyone liked hooves on women, then it would be natural, and not perversion. The only reason it 'is' slightly perverted is the bestiality aspect."

"Ok, I don't want to know about what animals you have had sex with-" I said.

"None at all, now that you've asked. I was hit on by a demon with a cow's head, Molech, but I didn't like it when he kissed me... Felt too rough." she said.

"...Um. Can we change the topic-" I said.

"*And animals can't kiss at all! Those 'perverts' are missing out on a good, human kiss. Hey! You should write that in your next email to the paper! 'Bestiality is a sin, because animals can't kiss.' Should turn some heads.*"

"...I... I don't send them anything, anymore. Should I?" I asked.

"*I think it's a good use of time. Lets you put your own views in concrete form, if anything. And anyway, why do men like high heels?? They're bad for the feet, and look like hooves! Makes ya think.*" she said, "*Now draw me, my artist, with my sexy legs and slightly perverted hooves.*"

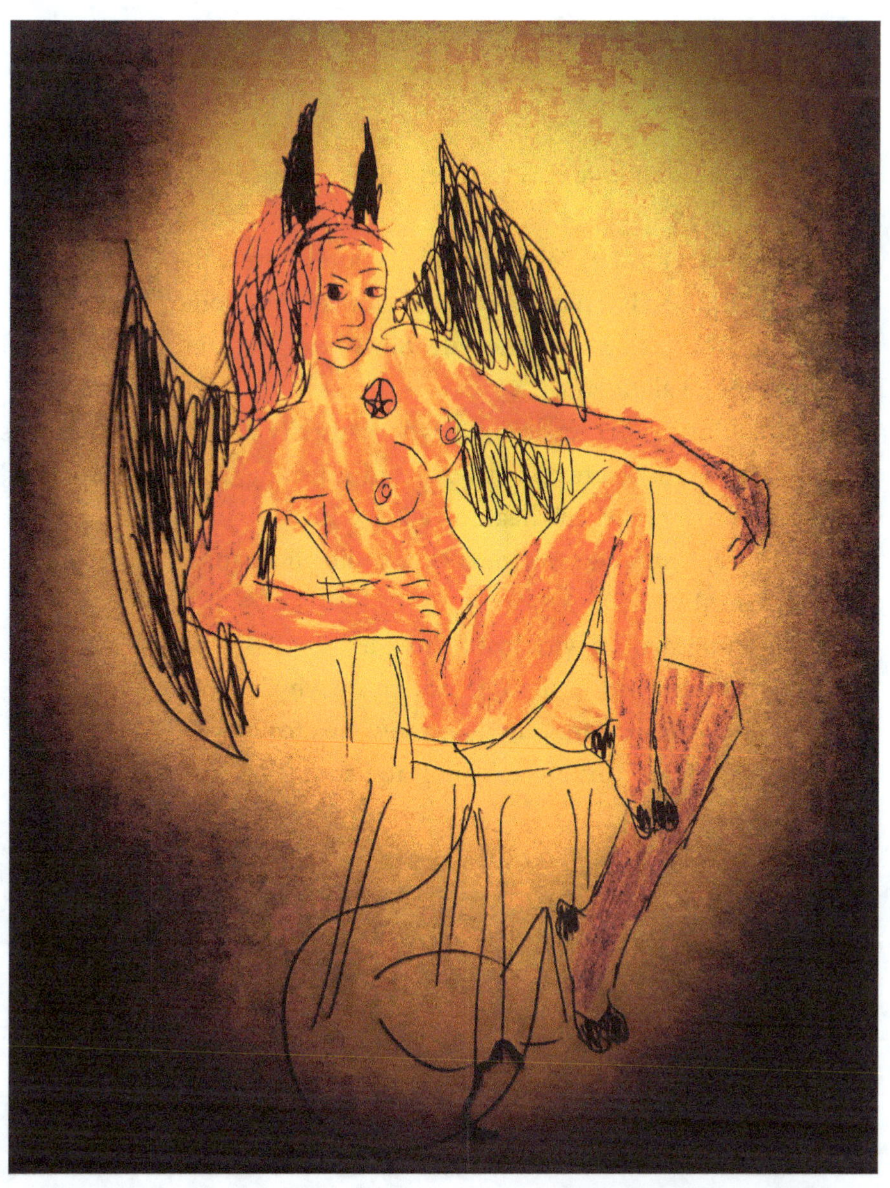

26

BAHGOD.

I am in love, and love is… beautiful. It is delicate, fragile… but I can only wonder why.

I am in love with the Devil's Daughter, after I drew her.

She is real… She is a natural unborn woman, like you or I-

I mean, she's just a normal female. She's beautiful, and I can only tell her that through all of you.

I feel like love is perversion, for who naturally has love? Who starts off with that natural, uncooked potato of a feeling? Love for another, who loves you. It makes my heart swell.

It is desire, lust, and sweetness of a smile all wrapped together in a concrete pancake.

It makes one swoon, with just a thought.

I do not understand it, and I do not know why it is happening.

But I must tell someone, anyone, about this feeling.

Even if you reject this piece, I am glad I could confide in you.

This piece was published by the paper.

I gulped and felt like my life was ending, when I read it. They put it in the art section, right above some beautiful poetry which was far better than this piece.

The Devil's Daughter kept on smirking at me where she hung out at the harbor.

I didn't know what to do.

But she took my hand, and we walked down the water.

"Love??" she eventually said.

"Um... ergm... I didn't-"

"Shh... You've said enough. I didn't know you felt that way about me! I looked at all your previous works, hating and despising me... Who knew love could be found in opposites? Besides everyone ever?" she said.

"...You've seen my other works? But they weren't published." I said.

"I was a snoop. I'll admit it. Now admit you loooove me some more..." she said, smirking.

"I- I lo- I just feel so tired, and I need a rest. I need a well, proper rest..." I said, rubbing my eyes.

She squeezed my hand, and said, *"I think you deserve it. You've been drawing nonstop! Take a breather, my artist."*

I realized I was squeezing hands with the Devil's Daughter. And then I began to worry.

Who else's hand was she squeezing-

She saw the frantic look in my eye, and told me to rest.

She led me back to her home, and said, *"One more pose, my artist, before a nice, deep, sleep... Draw me well... This is what the hand you held does when you're away..."*

And she- I suppose I should draw it.

When we were both done, she bid me to cuddle with her, and I fell asleep to her gorgeous voice...

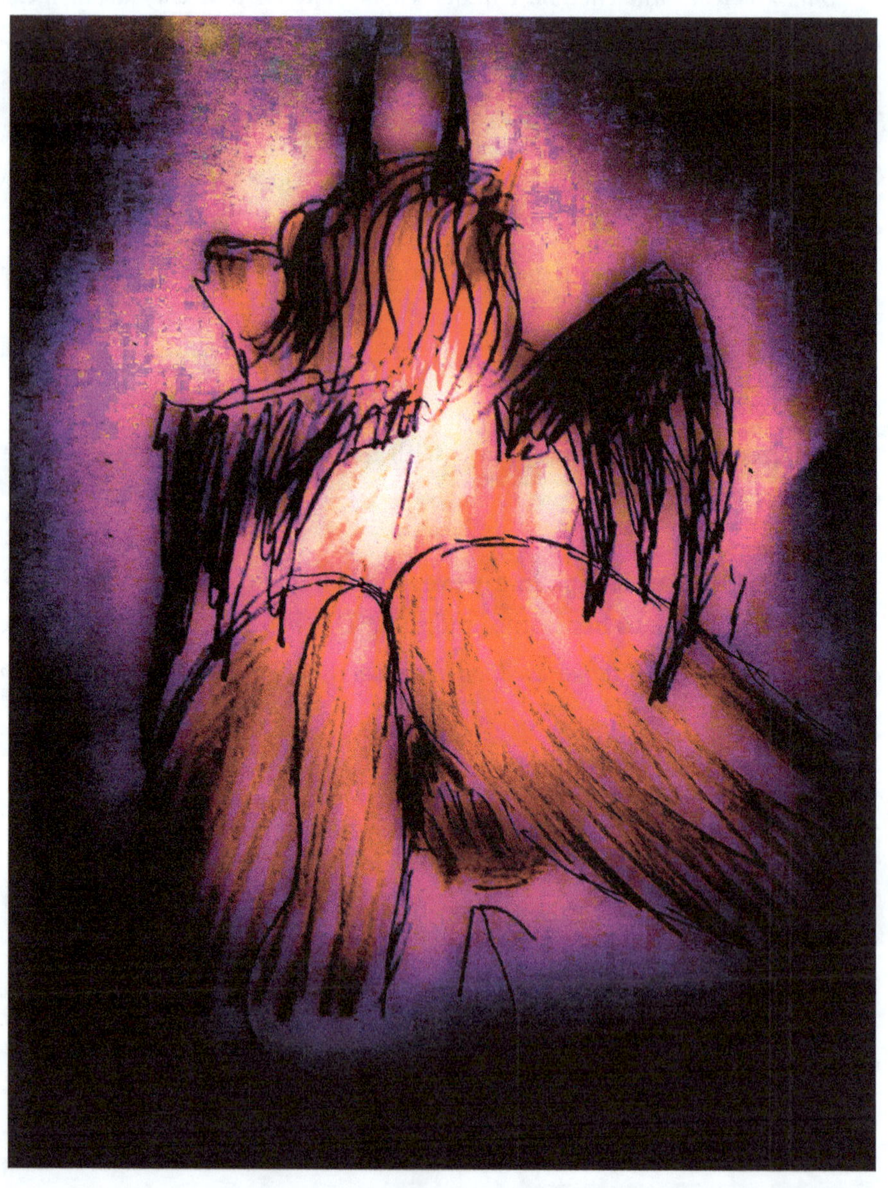

27

"I am what you call a succubus, dear artist. I am a demon of dreams and sleep, so you'll never really be without me, even when you think I'm gone." she said to me in my dreams, *"I can keep you here, you know. I can keep you in dreams forever, as my toy, my pet, my slave... Would you like that?"*

I had to think about it for a second.

"Of course it will be pleasurable... We can do things you can only imagine, in your dreams. What is it you want to do-" she said.

"I want to fly my bike through the sky." I said.

"...Ok. That's valid, flying is fun in dreams." she said.

She hopped on the handlebars of my bicycle, and we flew through the sky. I laughed in delight at such a feeling, the speed, the air, being so high off the ground without a care in the world. She was laughing too, and looked back to smile at me.

But then she fell off the handlebars, and in terror for her, I began to fall as well.

"Whoops." she said, and flapped her wings and flew.

Oh right. She could do that.

I continued to fall, worried I would wake up after such a thrill-

But she carried me in her arms, and said, *"We can do more, we can have the times of our lives here, in our dreams. We can make love in every way possible-"*

"What is it you want to do in a dream?" I asked, as she flapped further into the sky.

"...I want to be an angel. Like you'll probably be when you die. I want to be loved and cherished by more, all if possible. I want to be accepted, even if I'm 'the Devil's Daughter...'"

"I think you're cooler as a demon chick, though. But alright, I think I've got the hang of this... Hadn't had such a peaceful dream for so long!" I said, and laughed.

"But you nearly dream died." she said, looking into my eyes.

"I know. Most of the time my dreams are nightmares, so that's nothing new. This is fantastic!" I said, hopped out of her arms, and burst my shining white wings out my back, angel wings.

She crossed her arms, as we flew together, and said, *"I'm jealous. You've picked this up rather fast. Most don't even know I'm really in their dreams, and here you are flapping angel wings in my face... I... That's something I cannot do."*

"Why not?" I asked.

"Because for all the life of me, I do not feel like an angel. I am the Devil's Daughter, and I've accepted that over the love of God." she said.

We stopped to rest on a cloud, and I said, "I've got a present for you, when you wake up. You can really be both, you know. The Devil's Daughter and the angel loved by God. You don't have to be in twain. Rest easy..."

I kissed her, and I awoke.

She was still sleeping as I drew a picture for her in the morning.

28

"I look hideous." she said.

"...You do?" I said.

"This picture makes me sick. Throw it in the trash, because I never want to see it again." she said, crumpled it up, and threw it in the trash.

I left, sighing to myself.

I suppose some will always be a she beast. I thought- I thought we weren't just living a fantasy, perhaps not a dream in the sky where I was flying my bicycle...

I had forgotten my wallet.

Did she pick it off me?

I knocked back on her door, it was unlocked, so I let myself in.

"Where IS it... How... I just threw it out!!" she said, rumpling through the trash bin.

I looked at her, confused, and said, "Did you find my wallet?"

"By the counter, over there... I was going to give it back... I swear... Now what the fuck happened to my picture..." she said.

"Ever hear of wormholes?" I said.

She looked at me in fury, and I gulped. She straightened out her features, and got a beer from the fridge in the morning. She slurped on it, as I continued.

"Sometimes you drop a nickel, and it's gone forever... but someone else finds that nickel, *in a completely different spot.* It went through a wormhole, I bet." I said.

"This isn't time for your crazy theories... Someone stole my picture!! Was it you?? So caught up in your little angel fantasy that you rifled through my trash to get it back?? You really want to see me as an angel that bad??

"I swear I'll kill you, if I don't get my picture. I'm the Devil's Daughter, and I can do anything I like. I swear to MY FATHER I will slaughter you, torture you, unless you-"

"I thought you said it looked ugly?" I said.

"...I don't care. I wanted to burn it. Yeah. I was going to burn it, so it never resurfaces..." she said.

"Well, I guess it's good it went through the wormhole, then, right?" I said.

"...What if it comes out in a completely different spot?" she said.

"Maybe it'll give someone happiness. Maybe you'll find it in the laundry, next morning?" I said.

"...But then the colors... Everything will fade..." she said.

She sat down, started a cigarette, and I held her hand as she started to cry.

"Don't- Don't picture me like this... crying for an angel..." she said, whimpering and trying to wipe off her tears.

"I can draw you however you like. Anything. Dreams don't have to be just fantasies." I said.

She moaned, and said, *"Dr-Draw me... Draw me like..."*

"An angel?" I said.

"Draw me like a slut. Draw me as a filthy whore, I am one, you know. I'm just a monster... I was brought up to BE a monster... I- I-" she said.

I squeezed her hand, and said, "I thought that since day one. But you've shown me more of yourself than just the monster half."

She blew her nose on a tissue, and said, *"...Really?"*

"Yes! I did think you were going to destroy the Earth!" I said, and smiled.

She laughed, and said, *"Always an option."*

I laughed too, and we just laughed together. She hugged me when we had finally stopped laughing and I went home.

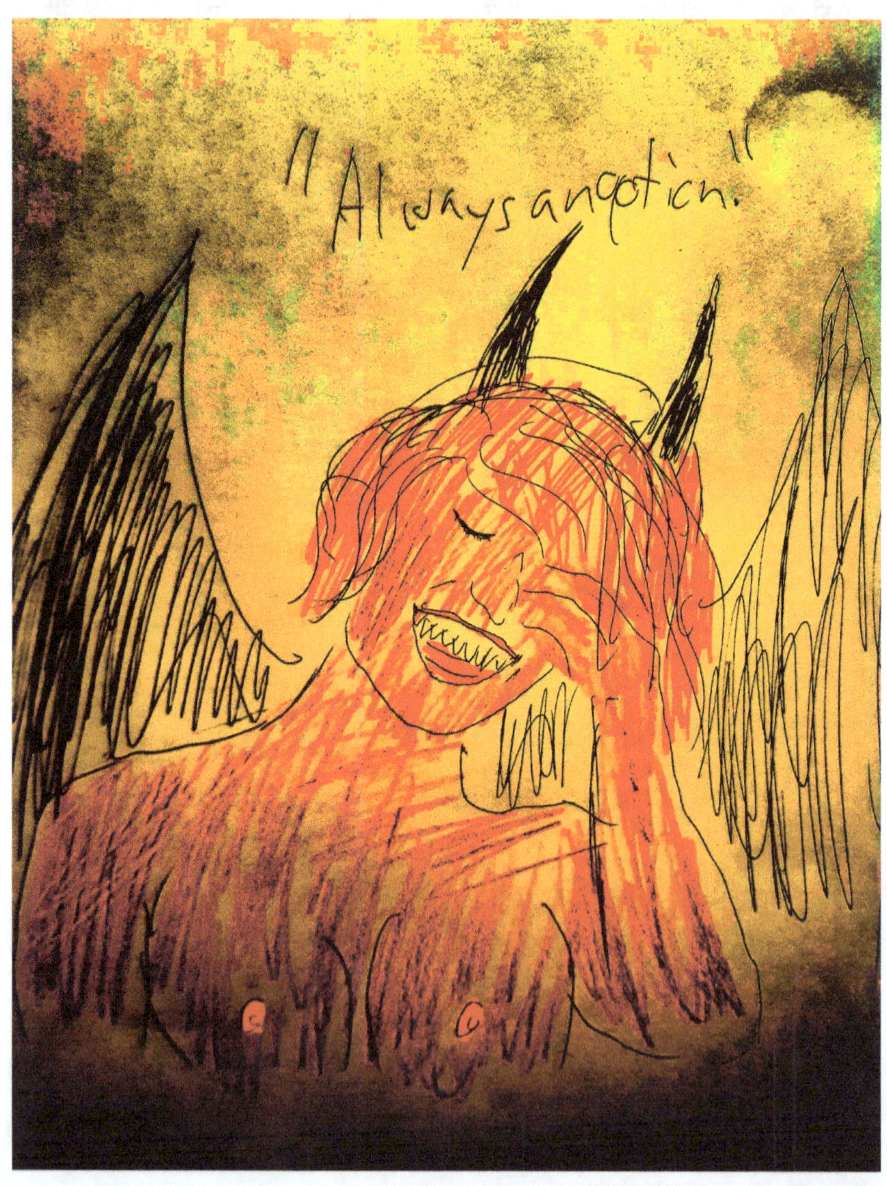
"Always an option."

29

I thought about her image a lot… and one thing bothered me. There was a seal on her chest, a tattoo I guess, that showed up sometimes, other times it was not even visible. What did it mean?

I asked her as we were getting lunch, and she said, *"My pentagram? Yeah, thing's a bitch. It burns if my dad gets pissed. He said it was a protective seal for me… But he has a way with words, and I never know if he's got some hidden meaning in things. Honestly it shows up more when I'm with you, but not always."*

I worried at that, thinking I was making the Devil mad because I was dating-

"Are we dating?" I asked.

She smiled, and said, *"Wanna?"*

"…I'm not sure. I suppose it would work, it would help me get my feelings… concrete. But what does your dad think?" I said.

She took my hand, and put it to her chest, and I could feel the pentagram mark burn like Hell.

I had to take my hand away after a second, because it was so searing.

"Makes him pissed. Let's do it." she said, and smiled.

I smiled back, trying to wipe off the feeling of intense heat on my hand, and said, "I am dating the Devil's Daughter. It's got a ring to it."

"Oooh proposing already? With a 'ring?'" she said.

"Let's not jump ahead of ourselves." I said, as we finished lunch.

"Well, I shouldn't have to say this... but you seem frankly quite out of practice at dating. I expect something, a little crappy gift of affection or whatever, to seal our arrangement. See ya, I gotta go help some artsy crew with their theater experiments... They're trying to make tasteful nude theater, and I'm going to give them some pointers." she said, kissed me on the cheek, waved to me, and we went our separate ways.

So... a gift of affection... flowers? She actually seemed to hate flowers, trampling on them if she could get a chance.

Jewelry? She never wore a thing.

I went to the store, couldn't make up my mind on anything, except hmm... then went to get groceries, and I thought why not.

I plopped the case of beer before her in the theater, and she said, *"Nice. Ok, you get a point. Not a concrete gift, but... I like it far better."*

"And I got you this! Something sweet!" I said, and proffered the stuffed animal to her.

She took it, and said, *"...A voodoo doll?"*

"It's a cow!" I said.

"...I can see that. Is this some hidden message to tell me to work on my weight? Cuz you think I'm a 'cow?'"

"...I just thought it was cute! And-"

She lit the thing on fire in her hand, and the poor cute cow burned to crisps.

"You lose a point, so we're back at square one. But let's not keep score. Ok, everyone! Let's see the rehearsal again!" she said, cracking open a beer.

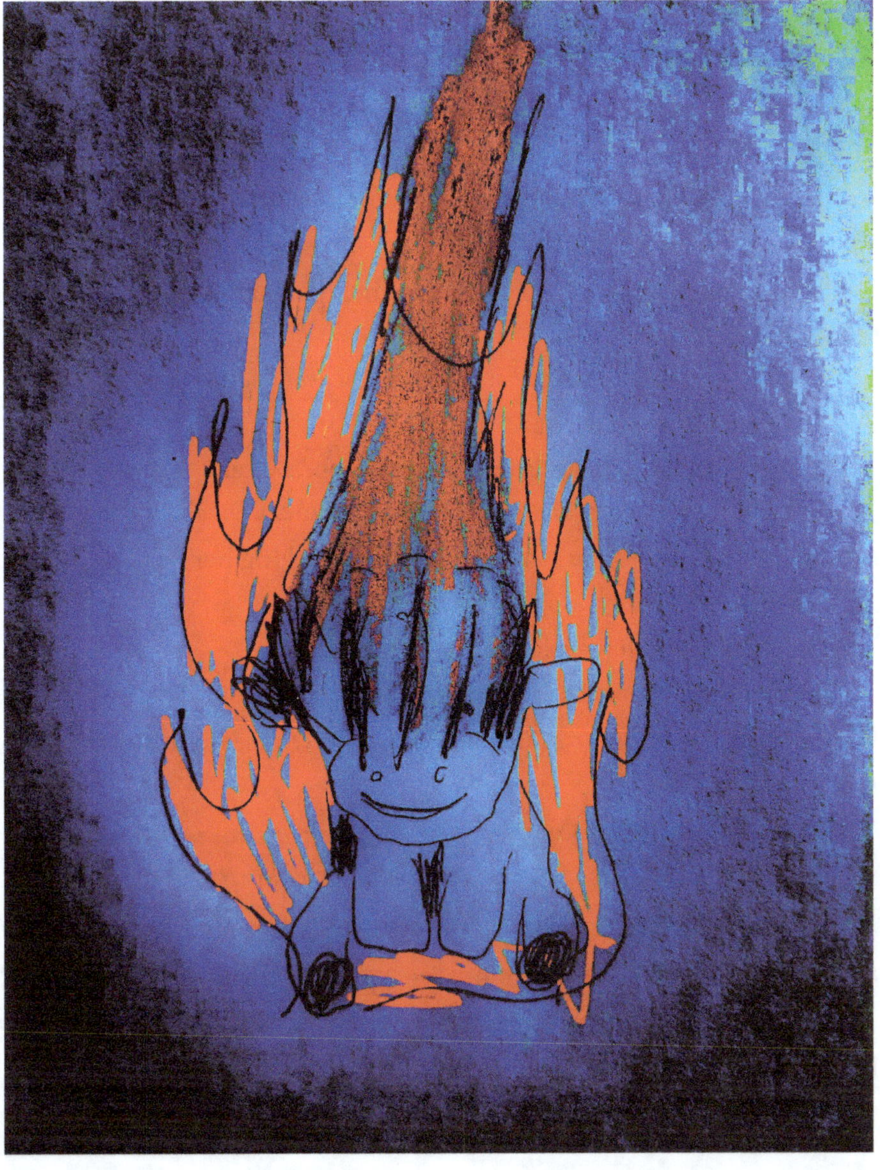

30

We were hanging out in my apartment, after she had drank the entire case of beer.

She said, *"Tellll meee about your passst. Ass. Your past ass. Tell me who was your honey."*

I mumbled, "Well... I made out with a girl and her sister in high school..."

"Fuck! Niceeeee. Did theeeey both giveeee you headddd too?" she said, stumbling against me as we went to the couch.

"...Um... No... It was at different times, too..." I said.

"Pfft. Dip in the honey and comin' back for more... Thaaaat's yoooouuuu... Good thing I don't got any sisters, eh?" she said, cocking her head to the side and smiling.

"I guess. Do you have a lot of family?" I asked.

"Jus' mah dad. I want to kill my mom." she said, almost losing her balance while sitting, *"Thanks for getting me the good beer. The highest alcohol is the best."*

"...I'm glad, although I wish you weren't so comatose-" I said.

"But that fucking cow. I told you about Molech, didn't I?

"Dude had the hots for me since I was 14. I mean, I was the Devil's Daughter, half human, and some demons really get a rise on that. My dad didn't intervene, when Molech came onto me, said to make whatever choice I want with whoever I want. He was never that lenient again, after Molech.

"*Molech was nice... I think... I was probably just a little girl who didn't know any better in Hell... I really thought no one was nice in Hell, and that I could do whatever I want and that people adored me...*

"*This guy was a god of child sacrifice, once upon a time, and I just wanted to lose it. I had those urges, like every teen, and looked at Molech's big, strong muscles...*

"*I suppose it didn't help being nude all the time, for the dude was always hard around me.*

"*And then... in Hell's fiery abyss, in a gas station actually, Molech and I bumped into each other, and he took me home.*

"*He kept 'kissing' me, with that cow's head... Fucking cows, I'm glad we kill and eat so many of them...*

"*And I had enough, because I was the Devil's Daughter, and I did not like being kissed down there by a cow.*

"*I lit him on fire, and his little 'house.' When I told my dad, Molech was never seen again, probably getting tortured by an even worse master.*"

And then she started giggling.

"*I'ma pose now, and you're gonna draaawww...*" she said, "*Oh! It's raining. Let'ssss draw in the rain.*" She took my hand and we went outside. She danced in the raining downpour, laughing, and said, "*I'm glad I could tell someone about that. Feels like a good use of time. Thanks for letting me burn your stupid cow gift.*" and she smiled.

I sat on the bench underneath a tiny roof, and drew her as she struck a pose. I smiled as I noticed no mark on her chest.

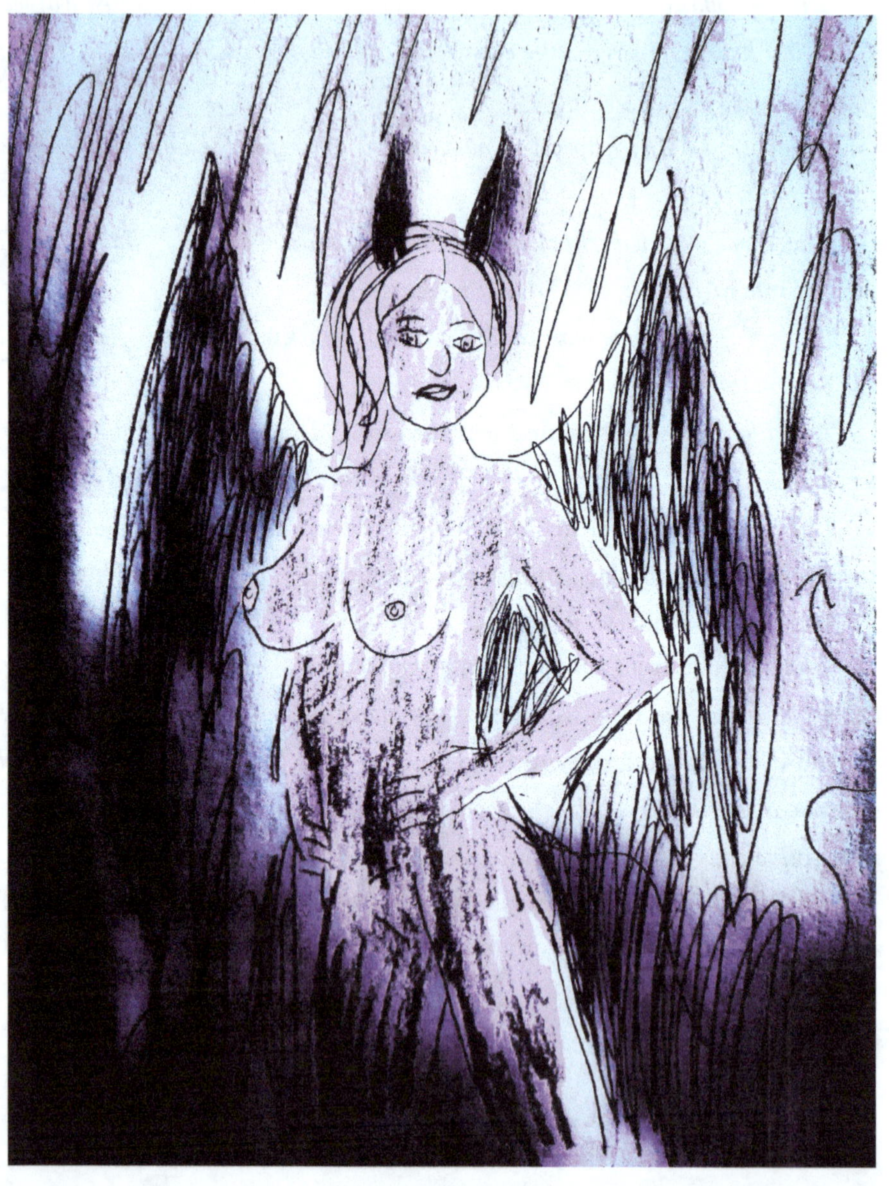

31

She slept on the couch, was sleeping in, and I thought it might be a good day to spread the Lord's good word-

Did I really have any say in that anymore? I was dating the Devil's Daughter.

It's not like I was dating her to change her or anything even. I just enjoyed her company.

I was about to take my trombone into the streets, to shout and play in ferverous righteousness… but the cops did hassle me a few times already…

I sat with my trombone, looking on her sadly. I wish I could hear Heaven's horns for real. I'm sure it would be marvelous, the grandest orchestra of music altogether, played from flying angels heralding the approach of the Lord.

I simply sat with it, and played some light jazz.

I was really getting into the thing, albeit improvising in every direction, sometimes using bits of other songs in my repertoire.

I soon was dancing with the trombone, playing righteous jazz.

I saw the Devil's Daughter watching from the sofa, and she said, *"Don't stop."*

I played for her, some more, playing jazz for the Devil's Daughter.

She sighed in contentment, when I got tired enough that I thought it was time for a break, and she said, *"I love jazz. My dad liked it for a while, but he really keeps up with the times to find the next 'Devil music.' It's become too accepted today, for him anyway, but I still like it. All I listened to was old albums of jazz when I was young... The searing rain of Hell burning down the house... with some nice Coltrane playing from the speakers..."*

"Coltrane's in Hell?" I asked.

"His music is. All good art forms go through Hell at the start, it's what makes them good. You'll never get recognition if you automatically start off in Heaven." she said, *"Can I blow your horn?"*

I offered her the trombone, and she took it, and played.

She actually played pretty great!

I told her this, and she said, *"What can I say? I'm great at blowing. Let's go to my place, and I'll play something for you."*

I said, "I guess we're good 'tromboners,' eh? Eh?" with a slight smirk.

She smiled, and said, *"It's cooler when I say it. Jerk off your tromboner on your own time, and let's go."*

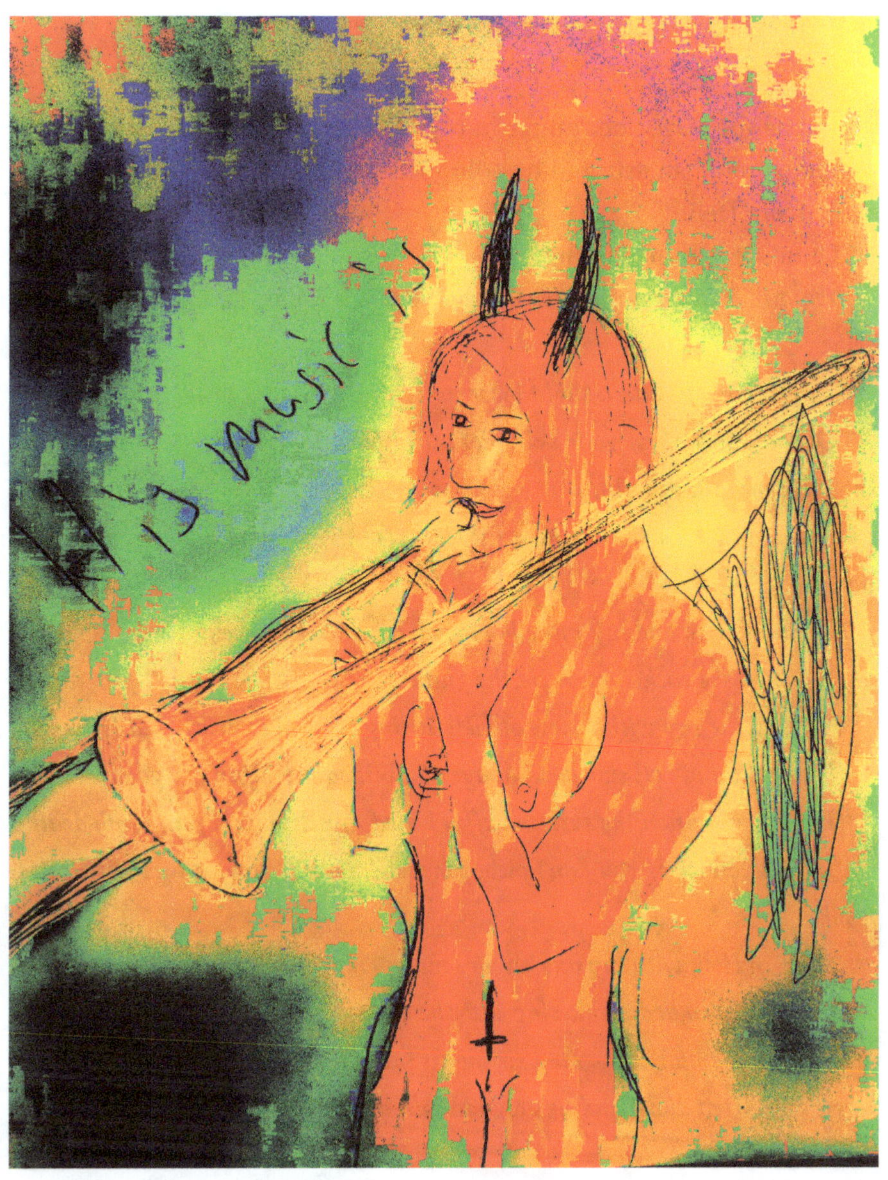

32

I sat as she thrust her guitar in my face, playing heavy metal.

She jammed an astounding solo piece, and I was in awe. So this was music from Hell.

Then she started singing.

"I'm a rock and roll star dead at age 12, I'm a badass bitch with my head in Hell,

"I'll kill you all with a slight loose note, please me well or I'll get the coat,

"Of oil to spread on your skin, hot tar of burning sin, That's what'll it'll feel like, with me and my kin,

"My dad's the Devil, you heard it right, I'm the Devil's Daughter and I'm oh so tight,

"With my axe and my mace I'ma smack you in the face..."

And then she rocked more on the guitar.

Piercing the sky with a note of Hell, lifting the veil of death and Hell.

"I'ma rock and roll star dead at age 12, I killed myself in my good clothes,

"I killed myself on the suicide cliff, I killed myself with a jump into death,

"I'll kill you too if you don't please me well, I'll kill you too and with you I'll dwell,

"Deep in Hell, with my axe an' my mace, I'ma smack you in the face..."

And she continued, climaxing into the end.

"There's one more guy, I'ma sit' on his face,

He's an artist dude, and he's a goddamn disgrace,

78

He's worse than you, cuz he's got no mind, he lost it all like me on the side,

He's an artist dude, with no real sin, but he's getting there quick, with one more fling,

With the Devil's Daughter, the master of all, she'll kill you too, with her axe an' her mace,

I'll kill you too, and we'll be dead at my place,

I'll kill you too, with my axe and my mace..."

And she thrust the guitar one more time, and stopped. I said, "What was- Ergmh… Got something in my throat. What was that?"

"...Did you like it??" she said.

"I thought it was amazing! I'm not certain why… but I felt like something was creeping into my soul with every note, barging in and banging down the barriers…" I said.

"Yeah, heavy metal does that. Cool." she said, and put her guitar back in the case.

"Although… you could work on the lyrics. Like what about…

"I'ma kill you too with one more screw,

One more bolt, straight into you...

And then you're dead, bound like a fool...

On my kitchen table, with one more screw...

"I don't know, but really try to paint an image or storyline with the music. My example was a little morbid, but maybe you like that kind of stuff."

"I love it and it's mine now. One more screw... to the kitchen table. Cool." she said, and grinned.

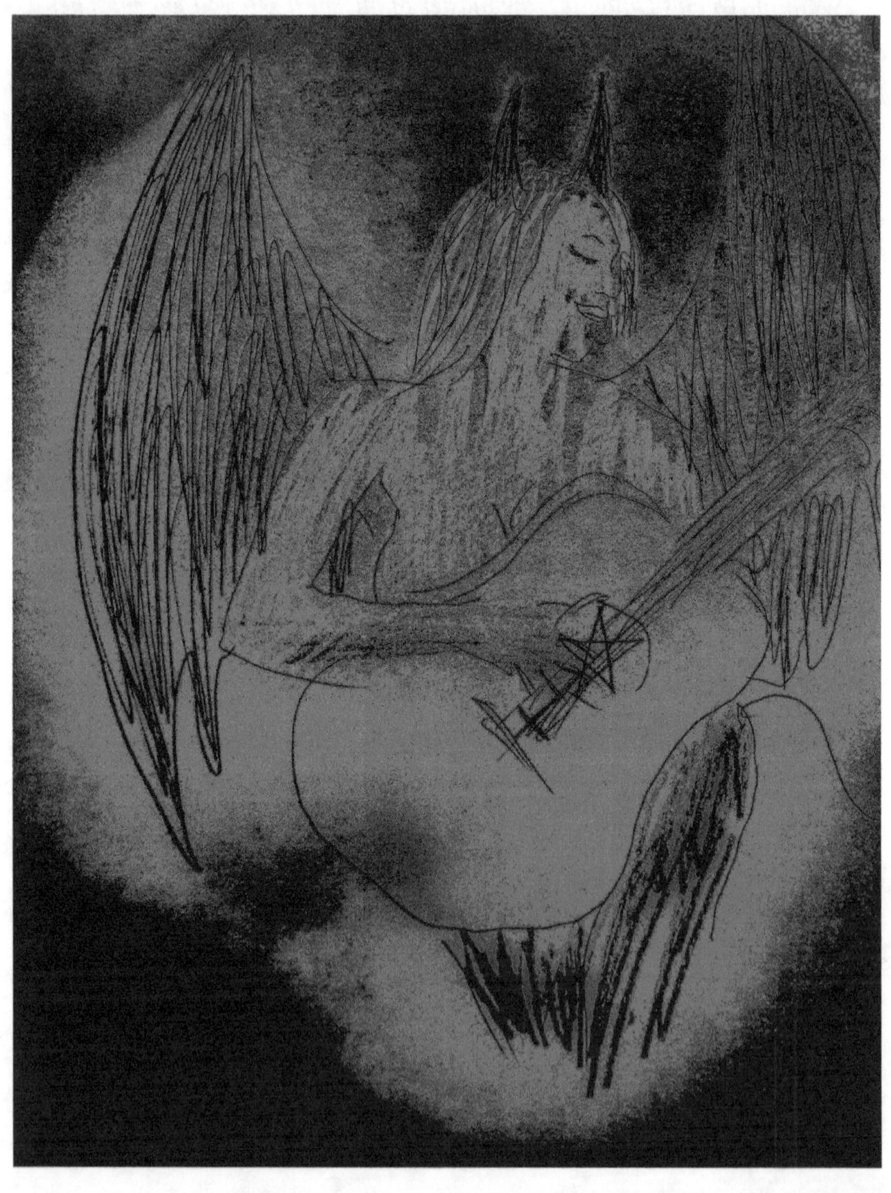

33

"Your dad treated you… right? Right? He didn't do anything… you weren't comfortable with? Physically?" I asked.

She shrugged, and said, *"He's the Devil, not some normal monster. I'm sure if he wanted to screw me, he'd screw me ten times over with no escape, submitting me to his authority with all my will at his command. He's a classy guy, and not about to rape a daughter he expects to inherit his holdings."*

"Oh, phew, that's a relief." I said.

"Do you think of incest a lot?" she asked.

"…No… I just am worried people are hidden monsters that I can't see. Sometimes that is sexual acts, oftentimes the most monstrous acts are. It is all violence in the end…" I said.

"I get that. Thanks for worrying, I guess. Although would you like it if I asked if your parents raped you?" she asked.

"I wouldn't, and they didn't, but… I have met with people who said they have been by their parents. It messes people up, gives them horrible PTSD and the like… It makes me sick." I said.

"That's ok… That's good, actually, that you feel that way. I wouldn't stress over it, however." she said, holding my hand.

"But what if it is continuing to happen? What if people's monsters are just around the corner, and worse they know they're around the corner, and have to meet them anyway?" I said.

"That's life. People always are suffering. It's why we've got such a population in Hell, because there are always monsters. You can't see them most of the time,

and if you look for them you'll see them everywhere, even if they're not really there. So don't worry about it. Those people who are hurting that way really just look for any sort of way out, and will find help if they can." she said.

"...I... I demonized the woman who told me... I was paranoid, crazy, and I thought she must be lying to take some sort of hold over me... steal my stuff... my mind... someway hurt me..." I said.

"Well, that was pretty stupid." she said.

"...Is there any way to be forgiven?" I asked.

"Forgive yourself. You only tried to protect yourself, and that is ok by me." she said.

I smiled, and the Devil's Daughter and I continued to walk down the street.

We hugged before we parted ways, and I felt the burns of the pentagram on her chest. I wondered what sort of monster the Devil actually was...

I watched her walk away, wondering what sort of monster she was.

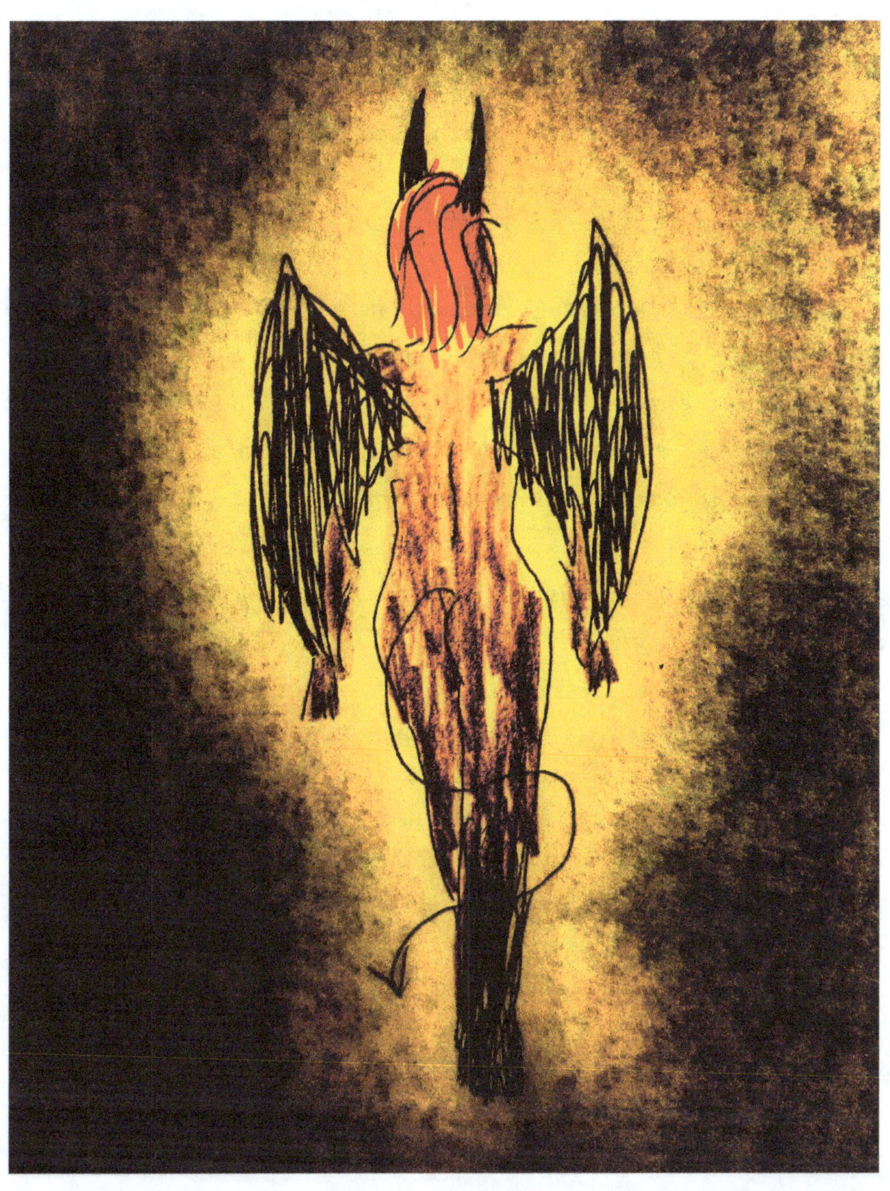

34

"Do you want to know why I haven't made love to her?" the Devil asked me in a dream.

"...Because deep down, you're really a good guy who is just misunderstood? That's a joke." I said.

"Ha. Ha. Because of a deal I made... with her mother. Surrree... God told me to love and care for her, and all that... but why should I keep my word to God?

"I decided I'd keep my little plaything close, my little daughter, even let her believe she has a real father. But her mother is a real soul, a living soul... who is bound to come down soon, as my weapon, my daughter, is on the trail of her now...

"I'd tell you to run, because you're next on my list. But we have you baited and trapped, seduced like a fly to honey-"

"Whatever, Satan. I'll say this, because you don't seem to get it...

"You're not the most powerful being in creation.

"Fear the Lord, or I'll start yammering at you like I used to do, and have a half a mind to do so again because it was so enjoyable." I said.

"...So... You gonna tell her what I said?" he asked.

"No, because I'm sure you'll wriggle out of it, like you're good at doing." I said.

Satan snickered, and said, "Wise. Keep your head on your shoulders... because someday someone may cut it off-"

I cut him off, and said, "Go fuck with some other madman. This one is insane enough. LALALALALA!! Jesus will come to SMITE YOU!! WITH HIS CROSS MADE OF STEEL AND GOLD!! REPENT, OR BY MY HAMMER YOU SHALL SUFFER!"

"...The good daughters always seem to go for the crazy guys..." Satan said, and sighed, *"Well, know this, if you harm her, I'll be coming for you. I mean that."*

Satan laughed, and disappeared.

The Daughter of the Devil came out of the shadows from behind me in the dream, and said, *"Aww. He said the last bit for my benefit. See? Toldja he wasn't so bad."*

I sighed, and said, "I really think you should rethink this 'kill your mom' bit..."

We sat on a flying bench in a dream, and she said, *"But I still want to meet her. If I end up killing her, then that's her choice, for not grovelling before my feet..."*

She stuck her hooves on my lap, and we sat back and smoked, her a cigarette and me from a pipe.

"You only smoke in a dream. Why?" she asked.

"It's bad for me in real life. I used to, a lot... but it's not good..." I said.

"Liar. I catch you smoking sometimes. I'm very good at hiding in the shadows, when you're in the back alley and smoking that pipe..." she said.

"...Sorry." I said.

"Don't be sorry to me. Be sorry to yourself, for not taking pride in your addiction. It's all yours, so keep it out in the open." she said.

"...Ok... I guess..." I said.

She snatched my pipe, and smoked it.

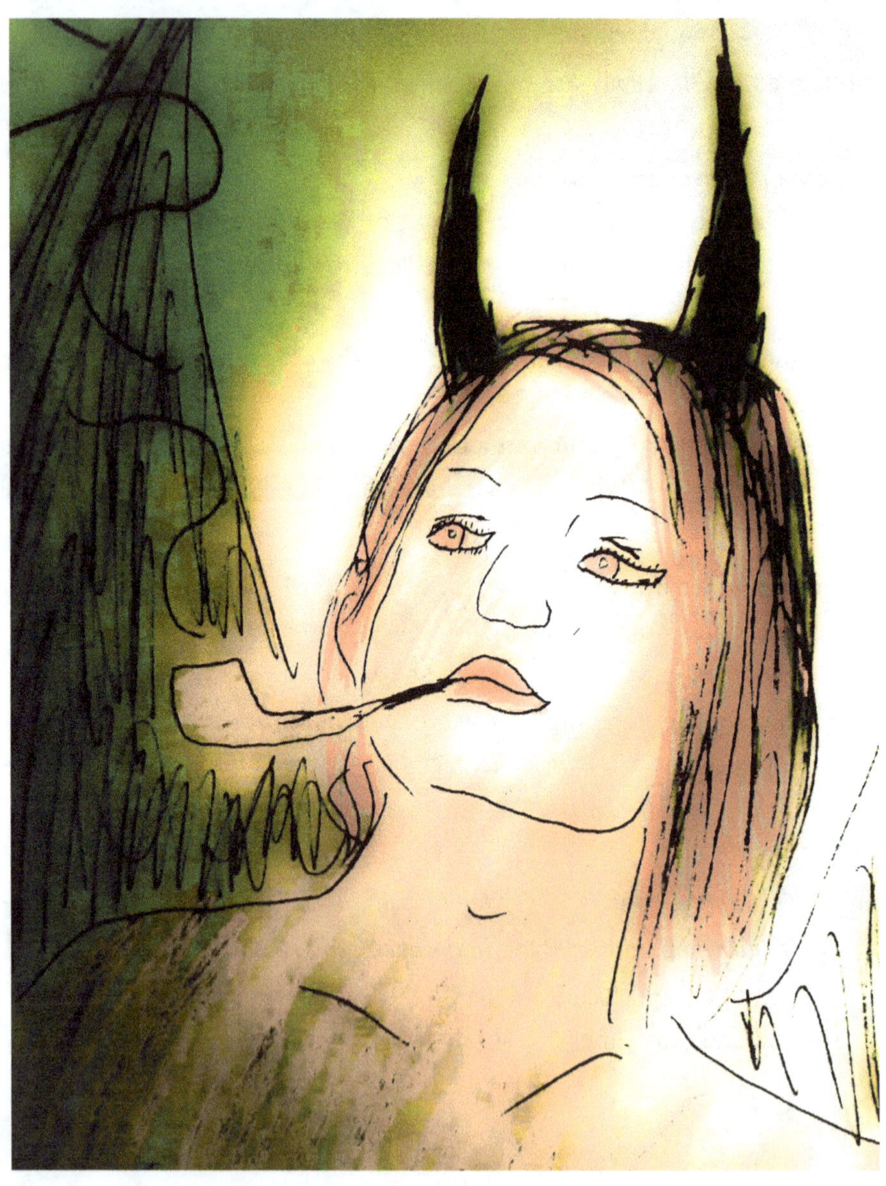

35

She put on clothes.

I said, "...That's... interesting! I mean... tasteful?"

She sighed, and said, *"You hate it. I can tell... Oh, why do I bother..."*

"No! It's just... You don't have to put up an act for me. Just because this is our first official date doesn't mean you have to get all gussied up in something you don't like." I said.

"...Says the guy in a suit." she said.

"I was actually going to be a groomsman in this suit, but I got in a fight with his now wife..." I said, as I took her arm in my arm and we walked to the restaurant.

"Lemme guess. Insanity?" she said.

"No... I just smoked a pipe, and she got pissed at me for it. Their house burned down during the bachelor/bachelorette party, and I think she got sort of suspicious of people, me especially because me and her never were totally best pals..."

"Whadja do? Flick an ember at her face?" she asked.

"No, on the ground, but when she asked me to pick it back up, I said she could do it herself..." I said.

"Yikes. You know women are the queens on their wedding days, right?" she said.

"But we were just all hanging out before the wedding day, as friends like we used to do. Everyone turned against me, and they were stoned and drunk, while I was just drunk… She hit me, and then went to hit me again, so I blocked and accidentally knocked her in the face…" I said.

"Oh well. Not like you can do anything about it. I'm glad you actually get to wear the suit for something." she said.

"Yeah… I sometimes miss those people, but not really too much. All my old friends abandoned me after I got into messy waters of my mind." I said.

"Hmm… But that's my favorite part about you! I think if you were some normal, sane Christian I would find you utterly despicable. Those guys are nuts." she said.

I laughed, then stopped laughing.

"What? You're dating the Devil's Daughter. You obviously keep an open mind, so open that even the rats get in there sometimes. I think it's great, and really makes me feel accepted. I could convert you to Satanism, maybe?" she said.

"…I think not. Truthfully, I know that Christianity has a lot of problems, but I look past it in favor of unity, in some cases." I said.

"Yeah, I take it back… Best not have you worship my father… That might lead to all sorts of messes. You'd be bowing and scraping to my dad… Disgusting. No woman wants that." she said.

I laughed, and said, "Yeah. Better off being subnormal crazy Christianity, rather than anything mainstream."

"Cool. Well, this is the spot. Is it too cliche??" she said.

"An Italian restaurant is all well and fine, in my opinion. Pizza?" I said.

"Oh, I'd love that. I really didn't feel like trying some weird dish and end up hating it. Bacon, too?" she said.

"Of course! You can't have pizza without bacon!" I said.

We smiled at each other, and entered the restaurant.

We sat at our table, and each got a glass of cabernet sauvignon.

"Yikes... the waiter is undressing me with his eyes... It's weird how you can wear nothing at all and people don't bat an eyelash, but as soon as you put something on they go nuts." she said.

"Want me to... you know... take him outside?" I said.

She smiled, and said, *"Thanks for the offer, but let's get our meal first. You can fight?"*

"Learned judo when I was young. And also wrestling, but that sport is not as tactical, in my opinion. Fucked up my knee in it, too..." I said.

"Hmm... Well, we can burn the place down, instead, howbout. Or dine and dash?" she said. A couple of people looked at her.

I said, "Um... Let's enjoy the meal first."

We got our bacon pizza, and it was exquisite.

"Mmmm..." she said, with a stuffed mouth, *"Nothing like overpriced, natural, local meat. You can tell this place does it right. Like, when bacon is undercooked-"*

"It gets this fatty taste on it! And also when it's left out for too long. This place just made it just now, you can tell." I said.

We smiled at each other. She winked.

I sighed, and said, "I want to address something..."

"Undress something, you mean?" she said.

"I honestly feel like you're too good for me. For probably anyone. My primal instincts scream out to me with your horns, fangs, tail, and even wings, but I can't help but draw close." I said.

"Of course I'm too good for you. Frankly, no one sees how great I am because they instantly see the predatorial aspects, like you mentioned. I'm trying harder, to appeal to your mind as well, if you can tell. I think you should take that as a compliment, and not look a date in the mouth." she said, and smiled, with wide open mouth showing fangs.

I laughed, and said, "Of course. It's just I haven't been on a date in a long, long time, so I may feel like I am unworthy of such a thing as a nice date."

She shrugged, and said, *"At least the food is good, if you're not having a good time. Let's get out of this dump though. I knew taking you to somewhere so stuffy as a lame, Italian restaurant would be a bummer..."*

"Oh! Yeah, let's go. Let me pay the check-" I said, but she grabbed my arm and we ran for it, as the waiter yelled at us, us laughing into the night.

"So you wanna go home now?" she asked in the alley.

"I actually wanted to take you to a place I know. We can dance?" I said.

"Hmm. Ok. Help me out of this blasted thing, though. I'm sick of clothes already. They grate against my skin and are wayyy too tight. I'm glad I thrifted this stupid dress." she said.

I helped her out of the dress in an alley. It felt strangely arousing, helping her get naked again, but I sighed in comfort when she was comfortably nude before me.

She swooshed the hair out of her eyes, and said, *"I was going to save that until the end, you know."*

"Too bad, because we're going to party with the scum of the Earth, the vagabonds, the hooligans the- Oh, they're just some squatters. No reason to hype it up, although it may be your taste." I said.

"You gonna wear that there?" she asked.

I looked at my suit.

"Here... let me help you take that off..." she said, and slowly, sensually, took off my suit.

Her arms were around me, at the end, and we kissed under the lamplight.

She untucked my shirt, giggled, and said, *"There we go. My rascally artist."*

We left the suit in the alley, on the ground, as we kissed again.

We walked along the water, like we sometimes did, and she balanced on just the edge of the pier.

We danced for a bit at the squat, and someone offered us speed.

I looked at my muse and she shrugged.

I was going to pay for the speed-

But then realized my wallet was in the suit.

We went back to get my suit, but it was gone.

She laughed on our whole walk back to my home.

We sat outside on the bench, as it started raining, and she said, *"Ever wonder how I pay for anything? I've got no pockets."*

"...I had all my ID in my wallet... and my money..." I said.

"And you never needed it for this entire date. Think on that. The best things in life are free..." she said.

"...Ok. Did you have a good time?" I asked.

"Always could be better. But I'm willing to have another go, if you are too?" she said.

"A second date? Sounds too good to be true." I said.

She smiled, and said, *"Maybe a few more, until we hit that nice g spot in romance. Wanna draw me again?"*

"Sure, let me get-" I said.

She kissed me quickly, and we sat for a long time, kissing on that bench.

She took me inside my own home, and said, *"Fuck the drawing.*

"Fuck the world.

"Fuck Hell.

"Let's fuck."

She smoked a cigarette in my bed, in the morning, and said, *"You'd think that would be the end, that you lost your soul to me when you've had sex with me, but the real goal of life isn't just sex. There is so much more to it than simple reproduction. If I wanted your soul, I'd have to take a lot more than just your body."*

I sat up beside her, and said, "I thought as much, but never really believed it. I thought you really were only interested in sex, at the start."

"Pfft. Any sucker can bang. It takes a lot more to have it be fulfilling. I think you were a little stiff at the start, but I think my tail prodded you into that comfort zone..." she said.

"Your tail... is really fun. I love to draw it, but I never thought I'd want to *sleep* with it." I said.

She wrapped her tail around my leg, squeezing it.

Then she wrapped it around something else.

"A morning quickie." she said.

I trembled pretty soon, as she-

She used her tail on me, as she smoked a cigarette.

She whispered in my ear, *"You can help me off later, too... I promise you this... I want to take you somewhere, oh, hot, for our next excursion into the g spot..."*

I had flashes of searing fire.

I heard distant sounds of torment.

I realized what I had done, and looked into her eyes that contained all of Hell.

"Only for a visit. There's some cool places in hot, hot Hell!" she said, as she tried to explain as I was aghast.

"...Only for a visit?"

"Cross my soul and swear to bejesus." she said, crossing her heart with a finger.

36

I swore I loved him. I swore I did.

But he wasn't nearly as nice as my artist.

All those pesky, little, teeny insignificant romances of mine... When I really just needed, oh so badly, for someone to draw me.

I broke up with that idiot person who threatened to be a real boyfriend, for my artsy lunatic on my walk home. Just sent him an insignificant little text, with my little smiley.

He was easy prey, anyway, and I'm sure my dad can finish him off.

That boy could never finish me...

I wondered at my artist's simple loophole... that he would be taken to Hell, "only for a visit..."

I wondered if he was as smart as he thought he was.

Wait... Did he think he was smart? He thought he was insane.

Hmm... I enjoy playing the wildcard. Nothing so great at having a game that turns you upside down, and then-

But that's my artist and my little secret, our last night's extravaganza...

I feel like the tide has shifted, for some odd reason. I feel very... exposed. I have hardly a notion why. I was bare skin, Daughter of the Devil, and I never played games of chance.

But... Why do I feel kind of bad?

Why do I feel like... like I've been tricked?

Wait- The artist wasn't the Devil, was he?? My dad always did play heinous pranks on me-

No... That can't be right.

It must not be right.

I am feeling very paranoid, as I walk home, and people- People are looking at me. They never did that before.

Someone is calling the cops. Shit.

I ran down the alley, as the cops blared their sirens.

A bum wearing a suit said, "Woah... nice ass, lady!"

No one commented on my nudity before.

I ran down the alley, as the bum hooted.

37

I'm not sure how he did it. Some of his art was frankly crap, but I couldn't even get a realistic stick figure.

I scratched it up and threw it in the trash. I couldn't get his features right...

He must've done something to me when he drew me. The spirits love to play with art... They love it too much. Something is fucking with me here, and it seriosly pisses me off.

I just huddled under the blanket, and tried again.

I scratched it up in a second. His nose didn't look that way!!

I mean, it's not like he got me down perfect, every single time, sometimes he even made my boobs bigger than they were, but I never really minded.

Hmm... What if I...

No, his penis didn't look like that.

What is it with stupid, fucking artists!!

I know. I'll upscale him with writing. That'll do it... He was so proud of every crazy little thing he wrote, and I admit some of them were funny... Did he think they were funny, too? Was it just an act, him playing the fool?

How did he do it... He started with something ridiculous.

BAHGOD.

Wait, no, I don't believe in God. Stupid bastard trying to take me away from my home...

MAHDAD.

Yeah, that'll do it.

MAHDAD.

...I didn't really know what else to write.

...Help?

Will someone help me, some spirit, demon, or hell, maybe a fucking angel or the big man himself up in the clouds?

I giggled to myself, spirits were always so quick to help me-

No one came.

It was only silence, and I stopped giggling.

I shivered, as I felt so disconnected.

38

I confronted him, as I was wearing thick black pants and a short top.

"What did you do?" I said.

"Hm? You look good today. I mean, you can always be naked anytime you like-" *he said.*

"Quit fucking around. Something is screwing with me, and you're the last person I screwed, so it's gotta be you." I said.

"...I'm not really sure what you mean, but I feel really good around you! I think being with you has been the best life choice I've ever made-" *he said.*

"I'm seriously pissed, and I'd light you on fire just to get over this, but I feel like that might make it worse. I'm going to-" I said.

"Wanna get a coffee?" *he asked.*

I stared at him, as I was frustrated, and I shrugged.

He didn't look very sinister, as he drank the coffee. I wish he did, because then I would know how to play him.

He chatted about his day, saying he was going to put together a portfolio of his art. A portfolio... of me.

In my nudity?! I suddenly had a pang of shame.

"Listen, what if we-" I said.

"No, it's really coming along nicely! I think I'll call it 'The Devil's Daughter Art Book.' Simple, but it really catches the eye!" *he said.*

"...You don't care that people will think you're insane, for drawing 'the Devil's Daughter?'" I asked.

"Well, what do you want to call it, partner?" *he said.*

"...Something not so cliche. How about- What about- I seriously don't know, but the Devil's Daughter thing has been done to death. I like fucking around with creatives, but not everything needs to be named after me." I said.

"Hmm... Ok. What about- How about- I'm sure I'll think of something later, please, tell me why you're so frustrated?" *he said, with a damn sympathetic look in his eyes.*

I sighed.

I guess I'd have to play the act.

But... who was playing the act?

Was it an act?

I said, "I just think- Oop."

My voice was getting funny. What's happening?

I told the damn artist all about my day, every little frustrating thing. People looking at me, gawking at my boobs and butt, when all I was doing was getting groceries.

I had to wear this stupid outfit just to get them off my back... but they still looked!!

"...That is odd... No one did seem to mind, before." *he said.*

"You'll never understand how annoying it is having people look at you, want to fuck you, with their goddamn eyes. I just want to pluck them out..." I said.

Shit. He was getting into something about his past life again. Why should I care??

"Well, when I worked with my dad at his restaurant, I'd get that, even later when I worked for a grocery store, and wore a big smock! The middle aged women do it the most. It is tiring, isn't it?" *he said.*

I looked at him sympathetically.

He smiled and winked.

It must be some hidden sign!!

39

Fucking got me into this, fucking will get me out.

I banged the daylights out of him, all during the day, and night too.

We fucked until he actually did hit the g spot.

I quivered, and quivered, as we moaned together.

I sighed after release, and smoked a cigarette.

Then I went to put back on my clothes-

Fucking, fucking, fucking...

"Yah... Yah wanna go again? I don't think it's quite out of my system yet..." *I said to him.*

"I mean, if you want. I was really hoping to draw you, though. You look so relaxed!" *he said.*

"I feel relaxed, but I really just want to- Fine. Draw me." *I said.*

I looked at the drawing.

I lit it on fire.

It was a perfect, absolute, masterpiece.

But I never wanted to see it.

"...Was it not good enough? I thought you really did a cool thing with your tail, just then, and I tried to capture it as best I could... I even got your hooves the most realistic I ever could!" *he said.*

I burst out crying.

He hugged me gently... and I wanted to kill him for it.

Never have I gotten such a nice hug.

*Some other bastards wouldn't even look at me, after we did it. But this guy...
hugs me.*

"You win, my father and I do it all the time. We fuck continuously, and I
want to fuck my own father more over you." *I said, hoping desperately he would
take the lie.*

"...Ah. You've never mentioned this." *he said.*

Nailed it! I was so good at lying, not even this guy could tell-

"But it sure makes me angry." *he said.*

"...Why?" *I asked.*

"It's just- *I want to kill someone like that. Someone who takes advantage of
their own flesh and blood... for sex. I swear to God, I'll fucking kill the Devil,
for you. For me, because this just makes me so pissed.*

"You know that's abuse. How could you not? It is the most perverted thing
anyone has ever admitted. It's sick, disgusting, and he's the DEVIL!

"I'll help you in any way I can. I swear. I'll never let that happen again." *he
said... looking so... furious.*

It really made me feel hot.

I said, "I- I'm sorry. That was a lie- I didn't- I didn't think you'd care.
I'm so sorry. Please don't think so badly of me... That never happened,
and never would. You're... you're not him, *are you?*"

"...How could I be? Dude has red skin, doesn't he?" *he said.*

"...That's a point. Let's... Let's get you something to eat, and I don't mean...
what you did for me, over and over..." *I said.*

"I found it enjoyable. I never knew... getting you off could be so fun!"
he said, and smiled, "Listen... tell me if anything like that does happen,
ok? You're not alone."

*I looked sadly at him, put on my clothes, and we went to get breakfast in the
middle of the night.*

40

"How can you feel so alone? All the time? Is it human or something?" I asked, as we were eating at the pancake place which stayed open at all hours.

"I guess. You mean you felt more connected to people before?" *he asked.*

He must know. I know... I'll call his threat to expose my lies... by telling the truth.

"I can speak to spirits, demons of Hell, even bitch at a few angels if I feel like it. There is no limit to my power I know about, because I can always learn more to figure out how to do something. I can steal your soul, in fact I was going for that, and bring you to Hell one step at a time." I said, crossing my arms and smirking.

He looked heartbroken.

He said, "I... I thought that, believed I *knew* that, at the beginning... I mean, not the whole thing with spirits and demons and stuff. Although the bit about learning is pretty human, we can do all sorts of stuff if we learn and try-"

I slammed my fists on the table, and said, "Don't you get it?? I am not 'we' to you!! I am the DEVIL'S DAUGHTER!! I don't belong here, I never did!"

He sighed, and said, "I wish you really could feel like you belong here."

I blinked. My eyes were getting watery. This was the part... that... This was the part that...

"Do you want to order anything?" *the waitress said.*

I quickly got pancakes. I got everything I could, and paid in advance.

He wasn't going to break up with me that easily!! Haha... Not after he's fed, and with a fully paid meal!!

I mean, how was I going to bring him to Hell then?? If he... decides to dump me? ME. The Daughter of the Devil!! No way he would do that.

He sighed, and cancelled the order.

He said, "I think we should each just-"

"No!! I- I mean it! Please don't break up with me." *I said.*

He said, "...I just thought we should each go home? Take a break from art, for a while? It seems to be stressing you, and I really can't do it without you, my muse. Just rest easy, because all we did... well, we just fucked all day! I am absolutely exhausted, and I'm sure you must be too!"

I smiled, wiped the sweat off my brow, and said, "Ok. I'll see you in the morning... sweetie? Should I call you that now? I really would like to take a break from the art scene."

"Call me-" *he said.*

I threw coffee in his face.

He blinked, tried to wipe off the coffee, and said, "...Good thing it's such crappy, cold coffee. I wanted to introduce myself to you."

I laughed nervously. I WANTED to enjoy this chase... I didn't want to have a name attached to a soul I would have to ensnare and devour... I just wanted him to be himself, for a while...

Would... Would I have to give my name, too?

"Call me the Devil's Daughter, anything but my name. I hate my name! Just hate it! So you can keep your name a secret, too! It's more fun that way! Yeah! It's mysterious!" I said.

"...You really haven't even picked up my name yet? That's... kind of heartless." *he said.*

Shit. That's true. No one ever never introduces themselves.

I sighed... I knew his name, I saw it when I fake didn't steal his wallet...

"I'm sorry, Luke. I'm... I'm... Jane."

It felt like I just entered a concrete relationship.

I wanted to take it back. I wanted to change what I said.

But I was Jane.

We talked some more, as I felt my world collapse.

I told him I was the daughter of Mary, Mary Jane, ha ha... I hated that stupid joke.

Even moreso because of what the name Mary represented in the Bible.

And I was the Daughter of the Devil.

41

I cried and cried when I got home. It was a nice day, sort of a second date just in bed, but I felt so awful...

My burns hurt, and I knew my dad was approaching.

He appeared before me in my apartment, and said, "What's wrong, sweetie? Not enjoying the hunt?"

"I HATE YOU!! YOU DID THIS!! YOU MADE ME TO BE A MURDERER!! A KILLER!! WORSE, EVEN!!" I yelled at my father.

"And I don't regret a thing. It's much easier with sins... let it all out... hit your father, yell at him, like your 'artist' did to his..." my father said, wrapping an arm around me.

I cried and cried, as he tried to hug me like my artist... Luke.

But he felt so cold, even if he was from the lowest pit of Hell.

He let me go, and said, "I am a real father, and I would never hurt you. Know that the worst part of abuse... is that it never happened. At least to the victim. The only one who says it's abuse is others..."

"You never hurt me... you never forced yourself on me... You've always cared for me..." I said.

"That's a good girl... Remember that, because that's what they all say... And who knows? Maybe it's true...

"But know I am the Devil, and they will try to tear us apart. They hate me for what I represent.

"This is true..."

"But... But you're the King of Lies..." I said.

"And what is a lie, sweet daughter?" he said.

"It is... diversion. It is... distorting the truth. It's not always-" I said.

"Not always what?" he said.

"Not always blatantly wrong. It's a scam, where you give them a feeling, and take it away..." I said, sniffling.

"And everything I've told you is just that. The only one who really knew who you were is that artist. But you've given him lie, after lie, after lie... But only you think it's true. You've lied to yourself." he said.

"You're making my head spin. Can't you stop playing games with me? I've always told you they're only fun for you." I said.

He chuckled, and said, "Sorry. I do love fucking with dummies in my off-time. Wanna play cards?"

I sighed... He'd cheat, like he always did, and I could never cheat better than him. He was ruthless, and never let you get a moment to win.

I told him I didn't want to play any more games.

I thought he'd be furious, but he started crying.

I asked him why?

"You're... You're finally not a little bitch of a girl. You've grown up. I'm so happy. Now go out and steal me some souls, because the games are done.

"You're not a toy anymore. You're my daughter."

And he disappeared in smoke.

42

I picked pockets, stole change from bums, cheated at dice and cards, took a man into a back alley under the guise of a prostitute, then turned him in...

Poor guy. He was so close to finally getting his kid back from his ex wife...

But I had taken souls!! I knew it!!

My dad whispered in my ear that all I did was inconvenience the lowest of society.

I shouted in anger! I did not need this torment!!

He told me I needed to do more.

I needed to take that artist on that trip I promised.

That one soul can make all the difference...

I asked him what he meant?

You're speaking to voices in your head.

You're speaking to the Devil in your head, Jane.

And really... someone else knows what that feels like too... He knows your pain... Why don't you get him to draw you with your bald vagina again-

I put in some music. That always drowned him out. I played heavy metal from my headset, and just banged my head to the beat-

But... the song changed, and I heard something remarkably sweet. Must've clicked it on accident. I was going to change it again but-

I just felt so calm, with this song I've never seem to have heard before. It was on my phone, it was in my library, but I never really listened to it.

I... I felt like... peace.

I walked to the artist's home, took off my headset-

And heard the heavy metal from inside.

He was listening to literal Devil music, songs which mentioned my father himself.

I knocked on his door, knocked again because he didn't seem to have heard and he said, "Come in! Didn't hear the first knock, Jane!"

"You can tell by my knock?" I said, letting myself in.

"Well, you go rattattatttatat, while others go, thump, thump, thump." he said.

I was expecting some horrid change in him, like dark eyeshadow or emo crap like that, but he still looked the same.

I said, "Why are you listening to this? I thought you liked jazz?"

"I like all sorts of music! Took me awhile to get out of my religious music slump, but I feel great listening to nearly anything! Except country. I don't know why, but I intensely dislike country." he said.

Shit. I wish he'd just lie, and tell me all sorts of fake bologna crap about himself. Why must he bare his soul to me??

It wasn't even that good looking of a soul! It was nothing special, and completely ordinary. What was the point of going for this guy??

Because you find something special in it.

WHY WON'T THE DEVIL BE QUIET!!

43

How would I broach this topic? How could anyone understand what I am going through?

I just said I needed to smoke.

I nearly ran outside again, and sat on the bench.

The artist came outside with me, smiled, sat beside me, and lit up his pipe.

I shivered, and he gave me his sweatshirt. I forgot how cold everything could be.

You were warm in Hell.

I needed to end this stupid voice in my head.

What... What was me, though? Was I... only a part of the Devil? Did I ever have anything myself? I used to find that comforting, like my dad was always at my side...

But now...

I just pulled on the sweatshirt.

"I feel like I am being intruded on. I feel cold, alone, and the wind is piercing my skin." I said.

"That's very poetic." he said, as he smoked beside me.

"It's just crap... I make shit up as I go along, I don't make beautiful things like you, planned for days-" I said.

"That's basically all I do, Jane. I don't really think too hard about what I make, well, I mean sometimes it takes planning, but most of the time I go with a gut feel over planned out battle plans. Sometimes that's all it takes, an instinct, over calculations. This is why I'm not an astronaut or engineer, though, ha… ha…" *he said.*

"Did you want to be one?" I asked.

"When I was a kid an astronaut, when I was in college an engineer. Never could succeed in any of those, though…" *he said, taking a puff.*

"But… Wouldn't that have been better than being a struggling artist?" I said.

"Probably. But I would be insanely depressed throughout it. Doing what I do now… It gives me happiness." *he said.*

"What if I took it away, though? What if I stole all of your art, and left you to the wolves? What if you had nothing but that feeling left?" I said.

"I'd still have the feeling. And I can make more. You don't lose something like this, well, at least until you get old and crazy with dementia, or die, then you won't need it anyway." *he said.*

"But you're crazy. So what." I said, but someone else was using my tongue.

I told him to stop.

He told me to keep going, and that a crazy soul is more fun to torment.

I told him to stop.

He said to use that tongue again, let him have a try, that he could do what I do far better.

I told him to stop.

"You want- t-to- I-" I said, but someone else was moving my lips.

"Are you ok? It looks like you're having a seizure. Like, really! I can take you to the hospital-" *he said.*

I started seizing on the ground, as Luke exclaimed in shock.

44

He sat by my bedside- He sat by my bedside.

He was going to attack me now- He was just worried about me.

He always hated me- He seemed to genuinely care for me.

"Are you ok, Jane? How long have you had epilepsy?" Luke said.

"I don't know… The doctors said something triggered it… *haha…*"

"Do you want me to stay? They say it'll be better if you stay the night." Luke said.

"Please stay. I mean- That's what he wants, for some twisted scheme! You must never see me again, *or something bad will happen to you."* I said, and eeped.

"…I… That's a very mixed message." he said.

I tried to read into my own words, trying to make sense out of them.

I burst out crying, and reached for him to hug me.

He did.

He sat long into the night with me, by my bedside, hugging me. I didn't want to let him go.

Because the Devil was at the foot of the bed, smoking a cigar and waiting.

Just waiting.

For one of us to give in.

You could strangle him yourself. He's grown weak. He hasn't fought in a long time. You could take him down… and that is all you need to do to come home.

I hugged my artist tighter, and shut my eyes as the Devil crawled on the bed, just above me, but not touching me.

I could feel Satan breathing smoke on my cheek.

My artist said, *"Just go home yourself, Satan."*

I opened my eyes, and saw my artist staring hard at the Devil.

Looking straight at him as the Devil moved away. The Devil went back into the closet. I don't know if he's still there.

I trembled, as the artist, Luke, looked back at me kindly and smiled.

"Are you some sort of demon, too?" I asked.

"Nah, I just learned from you. I really thought I was losing my mind, when I heard the Devil in my head, when I heard things that frankly shouldn't exist, talking in my mind..." he said.

"So... you really are crazy. I was hoping it was an act." I said.

"Yes, I hear voices. The medicine I take helps a lot." he said.

"W-Will it help m-me... Get rid of him? Just, I *love my Devil and all he represents but-* I just want it to stop for a while." I said.

He looked at me sadly, and said, "I don't know how to help you. But I'll do everything I can to try."

"What can you do about intrusive thoughts, though? They're just thoughts." I asked, almost desperately.

"Frankly, you use a bit of force, and a bit of acceptance. Heh... that reminds me of my parents, force and acceptance, Dad and Mom. You shouldn't shove the thoughts away, in my experience, but force your own will of mind, gently, almost peacefully, but with force.

"But you're crazy. How can I take your advice?" I asked.

"Everyone has their own madness. You'll find a way, an even better way, that works for you. If you want a reference... take it on good faith that I have survived this long, I should survive a lot longer if I play my cards right." he said.

"Not if you keep smoking continuously. That was the biggest lie you've told me, that you don't smoke, or at least don't smoke very often.

I smelled it as soon as I walked into your apartment, tobacco, every-where." I said.

"...I suppose that's true. Although I feel like I've got bigger problems than smoking. Like, I hear voices, and now I've got to watch out for my girlfriend, who's the literal Daughter of the Devil..." he said, sighing.

I smiled, and said, "I get that. You think... you can never mention that, for now? I just want to forget about that for a sec... Call me Jane, an' especially not Mary Jane."

"Ok, Jane. The big voice in my head isn't even always Satan, but John." he said.

"...An unfortunate coincidence. Oh well. John can screw himself. Hey, you ever use him as the butt of jokes? I call my dad- the Devil, out all the time on his foolishness." I said.

He smiled, and said, "All the time. John's a big dummy who smells his own butt. I know that's not a very funny joke, but it's funny to me be-cause I'm the only one who can hear his retort..."

I laughed, and said, "And the Devil is a stupid fatass with no taste in women. I mean, he fucked *Mary* for godssake, and not the biblical vir-gin. My mama sure ain't no virgin! She's a blasted slut at apartment E5 on Docksville street! She goes every day to the nail salon, like a dumb bimbo, then goes to an Asian restaurant and flirts with a server who's half her age! She's the dumbest cunt alive! And the Devil screwed her be-cause she said she was a virgin! Haha... That's all it takes! Tell 'em you're a virgin, and even the Devil will fall for you!"

He looked at me quizzically.

"Too much?" I said.

"...I think we should meet her. Safely, in a public setting, if you really feel so strongly about her." he said.

I sighed, and we hugged some more. The night was still there, like the Devil, and I just needed to be safe.

45

Luke allowed me to hold his hand, as we walked to the nail salon in the morning.

Mary wasn't there.

Luke allowed me to wrap an arm around his waist, as we asked the server of the Asian restaurant where she was.

She never came in.

I had a horrible feeling, and knew where she was.

I ran, and my artist caught up with me.

I barged into her home, where I knew she'd be.

It was unlocked.

I smelled the stink of my dad just outside the hall.

And I found Mary in a pool of her own blood.

I screamed, and Luke called the police.

They questioned us a lot, me especially… The cops wanted to charge us for burglary.

Luke was nervous around the cops, but plainly didn't seem to show it. At least tried not to show it.

They eventually allowed us peace, and Luke said, "I guess we got lucky… but they're going to question you some more, to verify your claims…"

I said, "I don't care… She was my mother… and- and- I- I really did want to kill her… but- but- I feel sad- SAD- that she did it herself…"

"The only reason we're not under total suspicion is the suicide note she was clutching… I… I think I need to… just… just sit, or something… I cannot sleep, after that… I feel awful… and I don't know what to do, and there is nothing I can do…" Luke said.

"C-Can you stay with me for a while? J-Just so I-I can sleep?" I said.

"Yes. Let's… Let's just sit or lay or whatever, together." he said, and we walked slowly down the street.

Eventually, the DNA test showed I was the dead Mary's daughter, and all charges were dropped against me.

They were going to lock me up for homicide, all sorts of wild theories that frankly sounded like they ripped them off from a wild detective fiction book.

But I was Mary's daughter, and she was dead, killed with a switchblade, by her own hand.

I read the suicide note… and it was very distressing. They didn't want to show me at first, but because I was the last of living family… they did.

I won't repeat the heartrending things in her own words. It is painful to me.

But she admitted to making love with a tramp, a simple vagabond she gave a cup of water, and allowed to stay the night.

There was no rape involved, she said, even though she called him her 'Devil.'

And that she aborted the child, for she did not want to be known as a tramp's lover.

But she admitted that the child lived.

She admitted I was alive.

But that I had disappeared from the abortion clinic, and was never seen again.

She took a long time trying to get all this information, and only found out years later… from dark rumors, to her own investigation.

I shook at this, that I was claimed by the tramp, her Devil, the real Devil.

She said she loved me, even though she never expected that I would read this.

"I." I tried to get the words out of my mouth, but the tears were too heavy, the lump in my throat too thick.

My artist, Luke, simply held my hand, and I squeezed it. He said, "It's ok. Don't try to talk."

I put my head on his shoulder, and simply sat with him, by the water where I first kissed him at.

46

"Mary Jane's Art Book?" I suggested in his apartment.

"I don't know, it *is* about you, but not weed." Luke said.

"Oh… fuck it. Just name it Naked Devil Girl Book. That's what it is, right?" I said.

"I don't know… I think we can do better." he said.

"Well, you're the creator. You think of a name." I said.

"Let me draw a cover, and maybe I can-" he said.

"Use the peach one. That really is the best one, in my opinion." I said.

"What if we try to make something even better?" he said.

I smiled, and said, "Get ready for some astounding artwork, then." I posed. I said, "I want boobs on the cover, so nothing stupid like little stars or something over my nipples."

"Heck, why not show the whole vagina and-" he said.

I laughed, bent over, and he blushed.

I turned back around, and said, "Something classy. You draw good vaginas sometimes, although other times-"

"That's because you're always doing something erotic with it!" he said.

I shrugged, and said, "Well, just draw me like this, then." and laid on his lap.

"I'm thinking something bolder… That's cute, but I'm thinking something really badass." he said.

I posed.

"Bahgod, that's like, really fucking cool. Tough, too." he said, and drew.

"And you just named the book, too!" I said.

"I did?" he said.

"BAHGOD, you did." I said, and smiled.

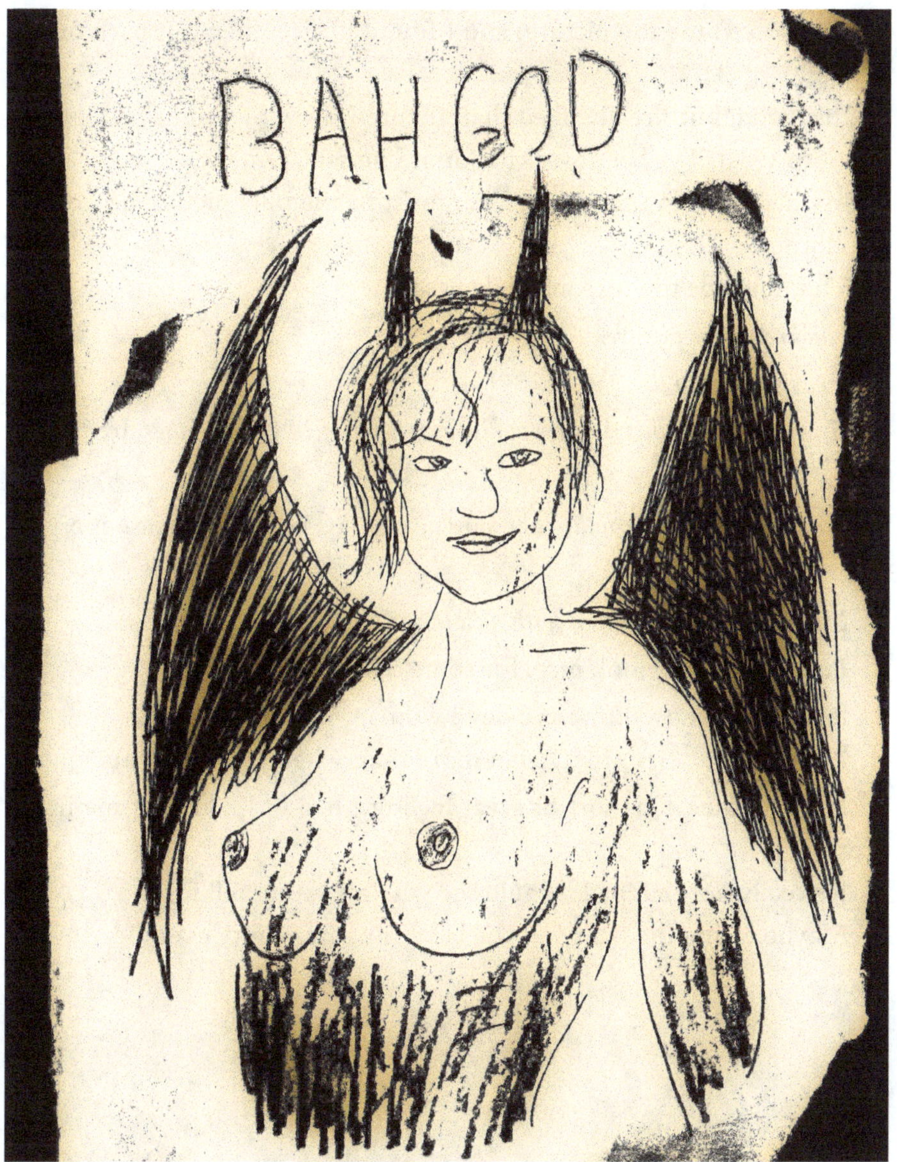

I felt like… I don't know. Clean? I really needed that extra sort of support from Luke, and then even the acceptance of my mother.

He showed me the picture, and I found it nice, then put back on my clothes.

"It's good, but I really liked that picture I drew of you in that dress... Want to see it? I've been working on it." he said.

My heart began thumping. That must be the only picture he drew of me clothed.

That must be the reason... I changed.

I looked at the picture.

I was so close to it.

He asked me if this was a good cover, kind of like the clothes are the outside...

I could destroy it. I could make sure no one saw me so... ashamed of my nudity.

I reached a hand out to it with a flame as he offered it to me.

But... I really did look nice, for some odd reason.

It blatantly showed me as a devil woman, in my black dress...

But I was so... *sexy* in it, even more than when I was ever nude.

Is this pride? This sort of great feeling I had of looking at me in my dress?

It's really not that bad. I could see why my father fell for it.

Maybe eating the fruit was the best thing humanity ever did.

47

I got a cat. I don't know why, usually I despised those smartasses. They think they're *sooo* cool, being able to traverse time, life, space, and be masters of everything...

But this little black and grey fuzzball was just kind of cute.

"You're a handsome little beggar, aren't you?" I said, stroking his chin in my apartment.

He mewled at me.

"Come on. Don't give me the silent treatment. I know you can talk, and I expect you to at some point." I said, crossing my arms and smiling at the cat.

The cat rolled his eyes at me, jumped on my bed, and cuddled on it.

"Aww! You're claiming territory! That's adorable... *because that's my bed, you little bitch.*" I said to him.

He winked one eye open at me, and we had a little staring contest.

I... I had to blink and rub my eyes after a second. This cat... lived a long time. Just looking into his eyes showed his godly experience in life.

I thought he may be even older than the Devil, if that's possible.

I mean, of course cats "die," to cut all loose ends, but they're never really gone for good. This guy...

Ohh. What should I name him??

"I'm gonna name you Poopy Star Shoot, ok?" I said, scratching the cat's back.

The cat rolled over, and allowed me to pet his belly. Fucking smartass. He don't care what I name him, he's just a cat.

"You remind me of someone I met in Hell. He's a giant asshole, like you." I said to the cat.

The cat purred.

"Yeah… they tried to kill him tons of times, but he wouldn't stay down. Even the history books tried to kill him, at one point, claiming his death by something or other… but I know from meeting him that's a lie." I said.

I expectantly looked at him for him to make some sort of remark.

"His name was Rasputin." I said.

The cat purred.

I shrugged, maybe he was just a dumb cat. I'm sure there are a few of those.

"Well, see ya, Poopy Star Shoot! I'm gonna get some clothes! I can't wait!" I said, smiling to myself, and waving the cat goodbye as he ignored me.

I threw tons of bags at my artist, Luke, and we went shopping. He sighed after I exclaimed in glee after every new, amazing piece of attire.

He tried to sketch every outfit I wore, as I asked him which one he liked the best.

He gulped. He was smart enough to know that was a trap question.

It didn't matter which one he liked. I wore them all.

48

I felt sane again, and I knew I was going to lose it again too. I knew this peace was only temporary. Jane seemed very happy, being clothed. The death of her mother was always fresh in her mind, but I'm glad she could find some distractions.

I felt restless, as the Devil gave her peace, and tried to fuck with mine.

I never felt so on the verge of insanity, but Jane gave me peace as well.

She was like, the coolest girl alive, and I realized part of my life revolved around her...

It's strange to think her end goal was to bring me to Hell, at one point. Is it still??

I am loseth my mind on silly pieces of my own fractured water, I must hearken to the Lord again-

You'd like that, wouldn't you.

One of them! Hearken! I HEAR ONE OF THE MANY MULTISCITUDES OF VOICES!

Multiscitudes isn't a word.

It's multiplistic dudes. Multiscitudes.

The worst part is I never know who is who. I know I am me... but who are they?

WHICH ONE IS THE DEVIL??

I asked Jane this, and she said, "...The dude with the pitchfork. That's my dad."

"But... But... they all have pitchforks! They all poke and prod and slice me like hay-" I said.

"Then they're all my dad. Give him a treat, and he'll leave you alone. That's what I did when he got pissed. I gave him some alcoholic chocolate chip cookies! He adores those." Jane said, and smiled.

How do I give a voice in my head a cookie??

I drew that silly Devil! HAHAHA!! I shall capture his form in my own hand-

He didn't have red skin.

He had a goat's head.

And then the next one I drew, he had golden wings, and was an ugly, handsome man.

The last one I drew he was an Italian plumber.

I sighed, scratched them all up, and threw them in the trash.

I tried one more time...

And the Devil was me.

I showed Jane this, and she said, "That's nuts, man. The Devil can change his form, and you've been you since day one. You'll never know what the Devil actually looks like, even I don't. He's kind of annoying that way... but when I try to remember him even... it seems hazy. Dude's a righteous fucker in magic, he probably created it actually. I'm sure if anyone could learn or create magic, it would be a fallen angel, right?"

I felt very stressed.

Jane saw this, and said, "Listen. Just don't think of what the Devil is, who he is, or where he is. If you look for him you'll find him, that's the trick."

"Oh. Ok." I said.

"I'm glad you can relax. Want to draw? That always calms you." she said.

"S-Sure." I said.

She posed in clothes. Like, barely any, though.

"Nothing I draw is good enough." I said, scrapping another drawing.

"...Just let it out. Draw something you enjoy, and don't worry." Jane said, and posed again, taking off her bra.

I drew.

She looked at it, and said, "...Hm. No demon horns or wings. It's... I don't know. It arouses something in me personally."

She took the pic, flapped her wings and swished her tail, hooves clomping on the floor, and added the pic to the portfolio.

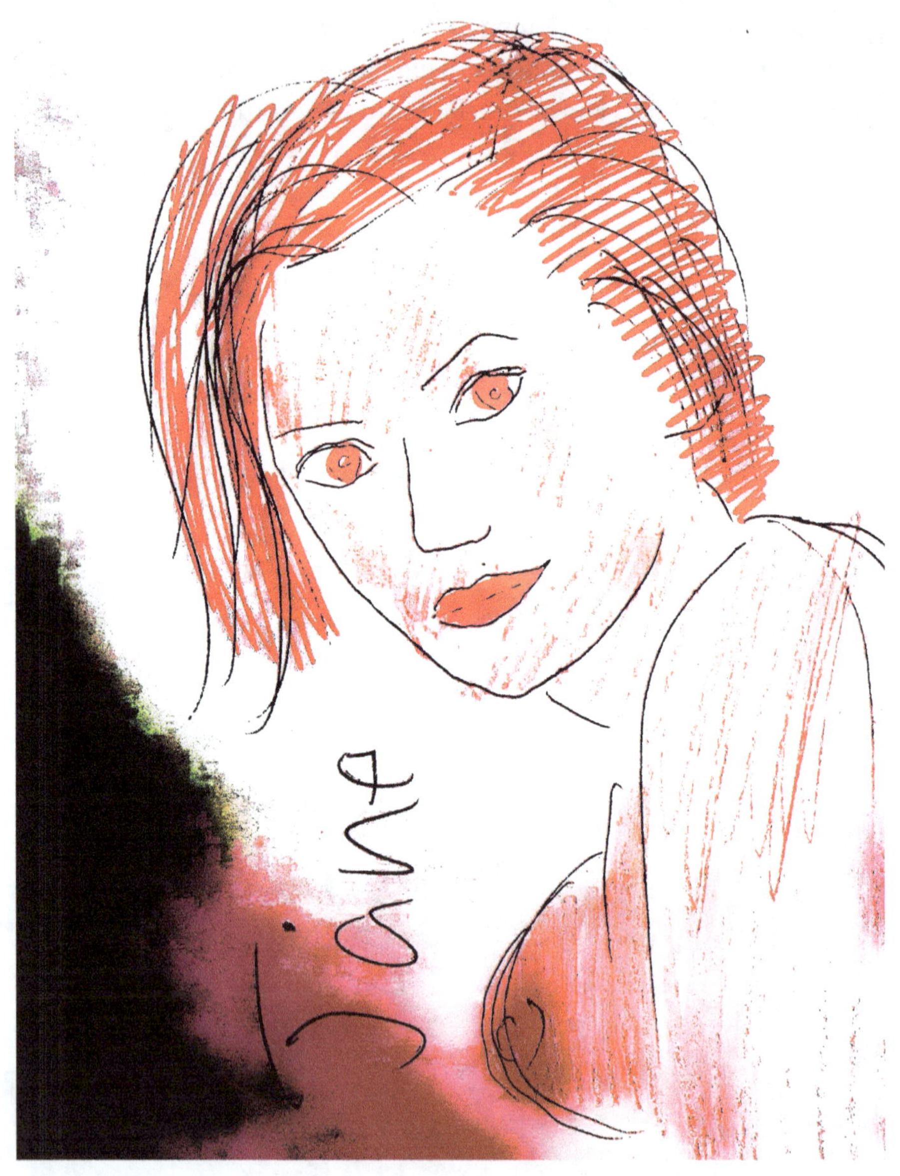

49

I wanted to stay with my artist, Luke, but I wondered at my dual aspects of life. I was the Devil's Daughter, even if I survived an abortion.

I was alive still, so where did I belong?

Did I belong... down in Hell?

I asked Luke this.

"I don't think so. I think you should stay in life for as long as you can, like any normal person." he said.

"With you? Would you like that?" I asked.

"I would." he said.

"Would you... want me to cut off my demon parts? Get a plastic surgeon who can actually see them, and have me be human? I'd do this, if you asked." I said.

"...No. I don't think you have to change anything. I find acceptance of your own body to be a marvellous trait." he said.

I smiled. That was the right answer.

So I bid him to draw me again, as I was.

He said, "...You look... Just a little depressed. That natural confidence you've had is missing. I mean, that's understandable, with your mom."

"...Wanna draw a sad pic? How do I pose sad? Boohooing? I don't know... I guess I am, sorta. I've never felt so... ugly, as when I put all this stuff on. I don't know, the first thrill of having something new is great, but after... I worry." I said.

"Just pose however you feel, and I'll draw it, my muse." he said.

He didn't smile, he didn't frown. He just looked at me normally.

"Alright, fine, I'll take it all off, cuz that's what you want to see-" I said, about to rip off my shirt.

"No, I think my best pics have actually been pictures of just your face. Do you want to just, I don't know, look at me? Whatever you like." he said.

"...That sounds boring." I said, "Can you be a little more forceful? What is it you actually want me to do?"

"Hmm... Let's do something trippy, howbout. Something a little abstract. Sound good?" he said.

"...Ok. How do I do something abstract?" I said, "Light stuff on fire? Like I can?"

"I'm sure I can picture something with the colors. What is it you feel like doing?" he asked.

"I want to be erotically classy. I want to do something with barely any clothes, but just enough to keep people wondering." I said.

"Wanna smoke a doobie? I mean, you can, I feel screwed to hell if I smoke weed. I'll just drink a beer." he said, and went to the fridge as I followed him.

"...You know I've been smoking weed?" I asked.

"Yep. Can smell it on your clothes. It's probably why you're so relaxed, but also why you're a little depressed." he said, cracking open a bottle of beer.

"Hmph. Ok. I'll smoke a joint, and you can draw that." I said, lighting up a doobie with my flame.

I snatched my artist's beer out of his hand and drank that too.

He finished the pic, and I looked at it.

"I *do* look relaxed. Not as trippy as I expected, but it's cool." I said.

"You're always so supportive of my art... Thank you for that." he said.

I smiled, and said, "For you, my artist, anything."

We then just chilled and watched TV. The dude didn't even have a TV before, no wonder he lost his mind.

We sat back, drank and smoked, with my hand on the inside of his thigh, my head on his shoulder.

Later, since we were kind of stoned and a little drunk, we got free coffee at the bank.

They tried to get us to leave, but we just bullshitted with them for as long as we could, drinking coffee.

I laughed, as we left at closing hours, and we held hands back home.

I liked being me, and I liked being Jane, not just a Devil's Daughter. I was Mary Jane, and me and my artist danced to that stupid song about dancing with me.

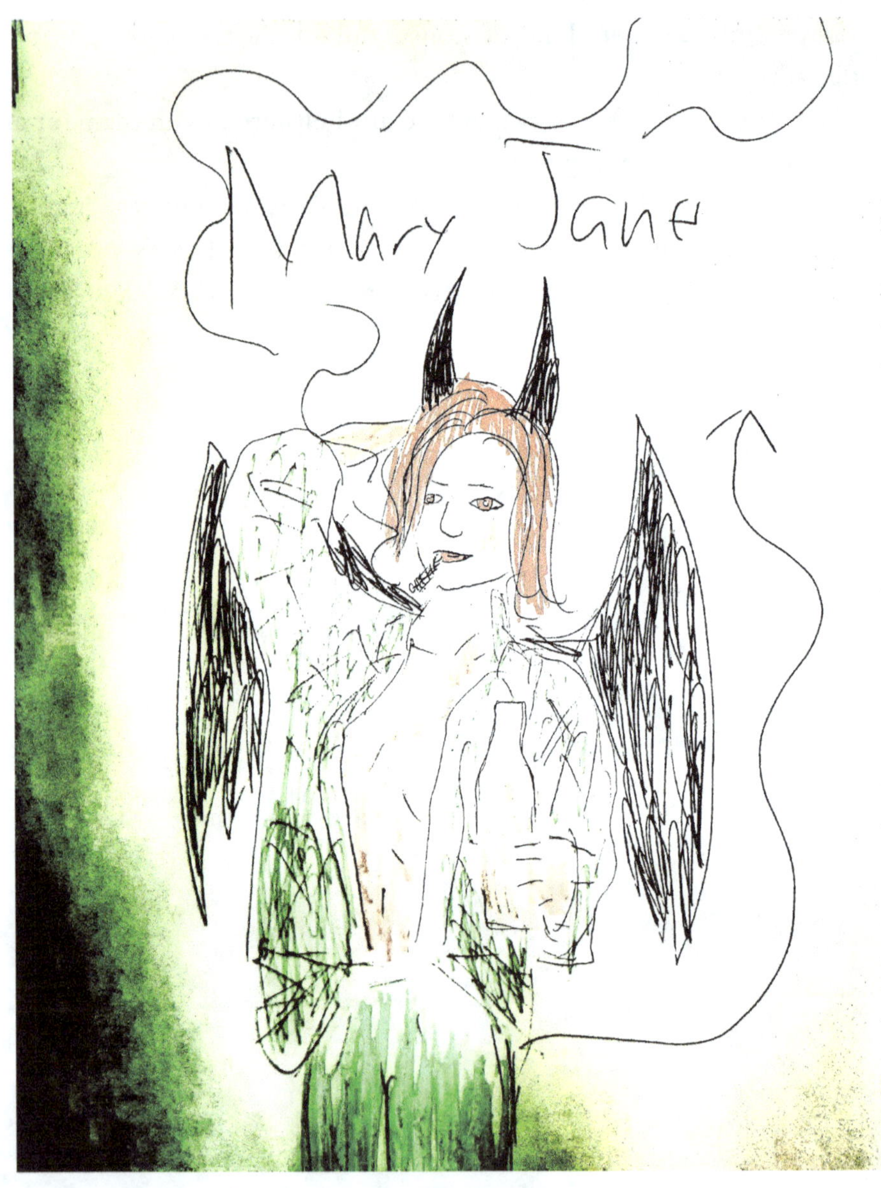
Mary Jane

50

He sure liked metal, in between the reggae, with a bloody mary in his hand.

God. This guy was the weirdest dude on Earth. It made me feel special that I found him.

My artist drank his bloody mary, and listened to metal.

"Listen..." I said, sitting down with him, "You know you're not perfect, right?"

He drank his bloody mary, and I knew this was a good time to bring this up, while he was tipsy.

"It's just... I want you to be more. I want you to-" I said.

"I can't wait to volunteer at that animal shelterrrr! It's gonna be so much fuuuun... Probably just cat and dog shiiiit, but cats and dooogs!" he said.

"You don't have to try and impress me. I want you to *really* be more. Not petty volunteering, although go for it if you like it." I said, holding his hand.

He stopped drunkenly grinning, and asked what I meant.

"I want to... Hmm... I want... I guess I want to kill my dad now. I like being here, and you've shown me new sides of yourself and life every day, but I don't want to go... *back.* I mean that. Fuck the puppies, fuck the kitties, my cat's a bitch, but I want to stay."

"...So what do you want me to do?" he asked.

An act. He was good at feigning drunkenness or madness, even when he was a little bit of those sometimes.

I found that appealing.

"I mean it. I don't care where people go, I don't want to be lord of Hell, I just want to be able to live… and not have someone claim me when I am going to die." I said.

"…What should we do?" he asked.

We. We were all together, all of us, anyway. Even if I had a bad dad.

"I'm very confused at this statement." he said, "I thought you had things figured out from the start? You always seemed so cool and confident."

"An act. What? You didn't think the Daughter of the Devil learned how to be a good liar?

"Let me inject some of my personal life into our conversation.

"When I was a child, my dad pranked. A lot. First one was a whoopie cushion filled with blood. He laughed his ass off as I sat on it, when I was crying thinking my ass was bleeding.

"There were others, but another big one was when I went to prom and-"

"Demons go to prom?" he asked.

"Of course. Prom is Hell." I said, "Anyway-"

"I've never been to prom, so I wouldn't know." he said.

"And hopefully you won't go to Hell, either. Anyway, quit cutting me off, and let me finish my sad injection.

"Anyway, *he* was my date. I thought it was funny how he- How he-" I said.

"What?" he asked.

"Kissed me like my dad did… Y'know, like a kiss before bedtime. That sort of kiss. And when I took my 'date' to bed, he kissed me like that, and it clicked. The Devil laughed, and told me, *'Love is a lie.'* Simple, but lasting words of wisdom."

"I don't think love is *always* a lie." he said.

"Maybe just a brief intermission before the end curtain, death, but love is stupid. I-" I said.

"Do you love me?" he asked.

"...I don't think we should put stupid labels on our relationship." I said.

He frowned, and said, "Oh... Ok. I guess that's fair, I know I didn't love you at the start..."

I felt heartbroken. Where was I even going with this? It seemed stupid now.

I tried to say it.

"I love you." I said.

I thought I was lying.

He said, smiling, "I love you too."

I felt my heart sink.

He was supposed to call my bluff.

And then for some reason, a bit later, I felt this oh so rising feeling of happiness. I couldn't really explain it.

I just chilled out with my artist, and we partook in stupid photography crap. Taking pictures of pears and peaches and crap, fucking with the lighting and shit.

I lay on his lap, and I felt sort of good.

Where was I going with this?

"When I was young, I was never really loved." I said.

Luke just kissed me, and it wasn't a kiss before bed.

Although we soon got into it.

51

I felt so good, with Jane, whom I… loved.

LOVED?? THE DEVIL'S DAUGHTER??

This was strange, because this was my own voice.

SHE'S SATAN!! PRACTICALLY!!

I had a strange feeling of paranoia.

I said, alone in my apartment to myself, "So?"

SO?? SHE'S GOING TO TAKE EVERYTHING FROM YOU!! ALL OF IT!!

And what if I want to give it to her?

YOU'RE A FOOL!!

I just really like her, is all, she's a nice gal-

-But only when she's around you. Really she-

I don't want to know, I don't want to hear it-

-She's going to get you, one day.

ALL OF THESE VOICES ARE YOU!!

I sighed, and said, "The only voice I can trust is the audible one, my own words."

THAT'S WHAT SHE WANTS YOU TO THINK!!

-She's going to kill you. And then steal your soul.

Please leave me alone.

NO! YOU DESERVE THIS!!

-This is probably what Hell feels like.

I had to take a walk.

I walked down the street, and…

I saw an angel fall from the sky.

I rubbed my eyes.

But she was smiling.

Smiling as she fell to the earth.

I tried to draw it.

I tried to make it as good as I could.

But I kept seeing this beautiful angel in my mind, and when I tried to draw her correctly...

All I got was blank paper.

I couldn't even start on such a figure.

There was no correct way to draw such a figure.

YOU KNOW THAT'S -That's your- *She's gonna...*

I ignored all of those voices, and smiled.

That was my guardian angel, my angel of war, and I'm glad she could enjoy her time on Earth like I was doing.

I felt blessed, and knew that she would always protect me, no matter what.

I told this to Jane, and she got a bit jealous, sitting in my apartment.

"Wish *I* had such a thing... *I'm gonna burn her eyes... WHO IS SHE?? I'll find her, and kill her, and-"* she said.

"Maybe she can look after you, too? I don't know, but I always saw... *her,* on a warm or cold Christmas Eve. She was always there for my family... sitting up there on the tree! I can't wait for Christmas. What do you want to do today? It *is* Halloween, for a few more hours." I said.

"...Sorry, I've been out working at the theater. Those chumps have had a rough day... But they should get the reviews for their nude performance soon. Wanna drink? That's all I can think of doing. It's a shame no one comes trick or treating around here, not that I *like* that... Idiot kids. I'd give 'em a switchblade- I mean... Never mind." she said.

"It'll be ok." I said, as she started bawling her eyes out.

"Why does anyone need such a silly toy, a knife…" she said. Her horns nearly impaled my eye out when she looked up at me.

"Let me get us some beer…" I said, and went to the fridge. There was one last cold beer and then a case of a new one. I gave her the cold one. She traded with me, because she liked my brand better.

We drank a bit, and didn't really talk. We didn't really need to.

But she eventually said she wanted to pose, and I drew.

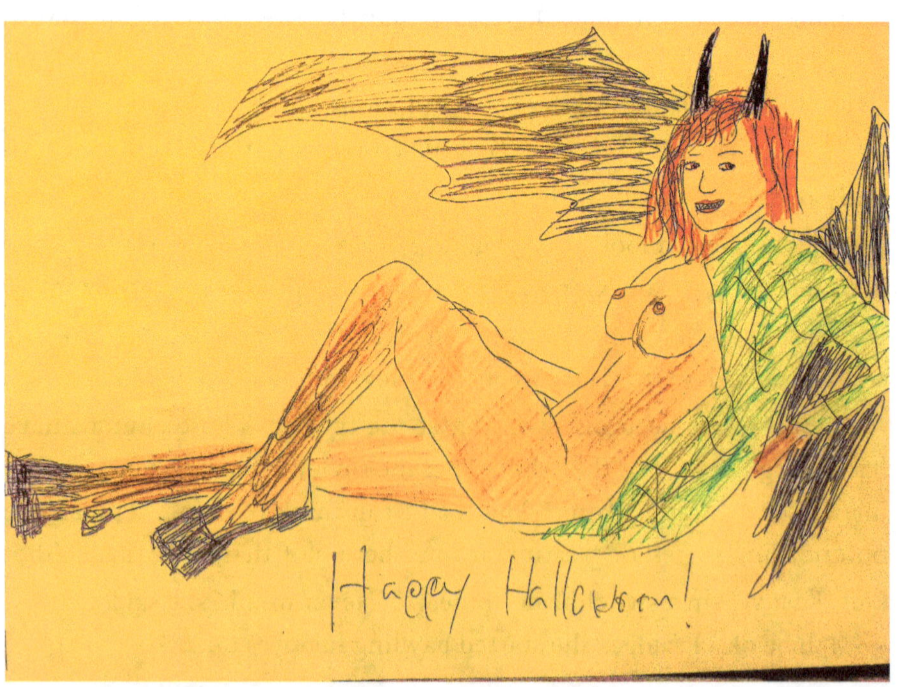

52

"My cat pretty much owns my apartment." she said, "Poopy Star Shoot is a giant dick."

-This is a lie. Cat's aren't penises.

"I'm having trouble with voices, Mary Jane." I said.

NOW YOU'RE TELLING HER??

"I think that's... well, healthy that you're addressing it. Maybe if you force it out of you, put it somewhere else, they'll go away?" she said, laying against my shoulder.

"But sometimes if I do, they fester, and brew up my entire psyche, like ROTTEN SWISS- I mean, like, they come out when I speak to you- *and I don't know what to do.*" I said.

"I noticed you've got three of them which piss you off. The last one was my dad." she said, looking up at me.

"...Who are the other two?" I asked.

"Beats me. Maybe psychics?" she said.

-That's right, I'm psychic-

DON'T TELL HIM THAT.

It's alright, guys, there's enough mind to go around...

I sighed, and said, "Wanna hear John speak? I can write him down."

"Talk to the voices in your head?? Fucking sweet, let's go." she said, as I got a pen and paper.

I wrote down John's voice.

Go to Hell, go sniff your own butt.

137

Jane started laughing.

"You... HAHA! You said that to him! I'm surprised he remembered! That's- That's fucking hilarious!" she said, laughing.

I said, "...But he's a real voice in my head."

"That just makes it so much better! You're great, man, and maybe it's a perk, and not a curse. Maybe you're, like, the luckiest man alive!" she said, and hugged me.

I smiled, as she hugged me. I never thought of it like that before.

53

"...I like Sisters of Mercy." he said.

"...So?" I said.

"...Aren't they weird?" he said.

"Are they?" I said.

"...Hm. I don't know. Would it be cooler if they were?" he said.

"Beats me. Let's listen to them." I said, pulled out my phone, and played a song.

I got it.

I really did.

They were weird, yes, the guy singing... *man,* what a weird voice... But damn. I think I got it.

And my artist just rocked his head to the beat.

And even if I played a cover song, Knockin' on Heaven's door... they put their own style on it.

I just listened, as my eyes threatened to break into water works, but I held strong...

For a while. Inside me, I felt like I was dying of loneliness, and all I wanted was to knock on Heaven's door, and be free, accepted, loved.

I just listened to the song, as my eyes watered.

I hugged my artist, and went home, still listening to the song.

I skipped a little bit of the ways, like some idiot kid.

I got home, pet Shoot, and said, "You're a little bitch with a heart full of gold. Gold shit. And I love you."

The cat mewled at me. Stupid cat.

And I knew this was going to happen today. Why wouldn't it? It was Halloween night.

I needed to be safe, with the cat, while my dad approached and my burns seared.

The cat mewled at me, as the shadows from the window distorted and changed.

The artist, Luke, didn't need to see this.

This is what happened on Halloween night.

The horror.

Rape? No… There is worse.

Murder? No… There is worse.

And it used to be my home.

The Devil appeared before me, looking like all the forms of evil he could, but I just saw him as my dad.

Be thankful, that your father is not evil incarnate.

He hugged me, and said the horror could stop. Was this a trick?

"Of course it is, sweetie. I'm going to rape and kill you now." Satan said.

"Is that a lie?" I asked.

"Of course it is, sweetie. I would never do that." Lucifer said.

"What do you want?" I asked.

"I want you to have a happy Halloween. What do you take me for? Some sort of monster?" the Devil said, and laughed.

"…Yes." I said.

"That's fair. I did always put used tampons in your coffee, when you got into drinking them…" he said.

"…But you're a guy." I said.

"You're not." he said, and snickered.

"Ok, quit the shit. That stuff was cute when I was growing up, but now it's stupid." I said.

"I really don't know what to say to you. You've even grown past your fa-ther..." Satan said, *"MAYBE YOU SHOULD KILL THE ARTIST. I am your master-"*

The cat mewled, and the Devil looked at him.

"...You got a cat?" the Devil said.

The cat said, "Yes, she did, and I seriously don't like breaking the fourth wall here, but you kind of put me on the spot, and I will play the part.

"There is no master of the universe, not even God, not the Devil, not even me.

"We've always been free, every demon and angel, even stupid humans who name me stupid names.

"And you realize this, as you read, that you are not the most powerful being in creation.

"No one is. So take your pranks elsewhere, and leave my stupid human- I mean, weird demon girl, alone."

"That's why I got a cat." I said.

My dad laughed, and said, *"Good. I hope you keep safe, for the times to come. Do you need any cash?"*

"No, cuz you're broke. *Just go home, Dad."* I said.

"...That's a good girl, looking at the truth... See ya!" my dad said, and disappeared in smoke.

I pet the cat. He seemed so big, but was just a cat.

Of course he was a cat.

Everyone just megalomanias sometimes, thinking they're the strongest ever... but not a cat.

The cat purred in my arms.

54

Goddamn cats. I swear he just jumped through time. Sometimes he did stuff in my past I wasn't sure about in my future, even though I had only just gotten him a week ago.

The cat invited me to follow him, in his next extravaganza through time.

I saw Luke nearly attempt suicide, almost jumping off the cliff.

I watched as Luke cut his wrists, in heartbreak.

And I saw him flirt with me, although…

Was I death? Was I another suicide option?

The cat said, "No, he just likes you. Why should he do that?"

I said, "Because I'm the Daughter of the Devil? He gets a rise of that, I bet."

"It's a perk, without a doubt, but really… I think he's just lonely. I was a friend of his previous cat, who is resting in the ground for a few eternities… And he's got really no one else." the cat said.

"Oh… So should I be an even better friend?" I said.

"You can always try. I'd give him-" the cat said.

"Space?" I said.

"That may be like a jump into the ocean for him." the cat said.

"…Is that a good or a bad thing?" I said.

"You decide… I'm tired, so piss off and get off my bed…" the cat said, as we got to the bed.

I smiled, and said, *"You little cunt. You're Poopy Star Shoot, and really just a cat-"*

The cat said, "Oh, bother someone else with your demon voice. Just piss off…"

I shrugged.

I got Luke some flowers.

"…Thanks?" he said.

"Isn't that what you're supposed to give someone you like? Flowers?" I said.

"…Um… Usually only the girls get flowers…" he said, looking at the things.

"Aren't they great, though?? Red roses!" I said, smiling.

"…I suppose. Yes! They're great. Although I really would just like a beer, honestly. This is a very classy gift, though…" he said.

I smiled. He liked them.

"Now wanna… Wanna pose with them? And I can draw you?" I asked.

"…Huh? I thought you hated drawing." he said.

"Do… Do something… nude with them. Please!" I said.

He said, "…Ok. Um, alright. I'll get on the bed?"

"Just like that. Yes… Like that." I said, as he undressed and then posed.

I smiled, as he posed in a rather ridiculous manner.

I sketched it as best I could.

It really wasn't that good, but it was mine.

I soon picked the flowers off… off of him… and let him have some fun…

I didn't like that he was nearly a suicide case, too.

So, I gave him some life…

In… In multiple ways…

You know this is a stupid joke. Just an act.

You know you're going to wake up tomorrow and feel ashamed.

You know this is ridiculous, especially that pose-

Shh. I'm about to-

Ahh.

Better, for both of us, quite actually.

I lay beside my artist and smoked a cigarette.

55

This has to end sometime.

You're prolonging it, giving her false hope.

Shh... This is better for both of us.

I think.

I KNOW.

I AM JESUS CHRIST ALMIGHTY-

No, that's not right. I sure am not almighty.

I sang to get the craziness out of me.

"I hope you wanna die in a goddamn fire, cuz I hate you the most,

I hope you wanna die in a goddamn pyre, when you get fuckin toast,

I hope you wanna die cuz I hate you too you're the worst thing ever now,

I hope you wanna die like a goddamn monkey in the zoo,

I hate you all and you especially and hope you die like me..."

"That was beautiful." Jane said, from the windowsill.

I looked over at her, and sighed. I tried to straighten myself and opened the window for her. She flapped inside, and hugged me.

My cheek was twitching.

"I like that you hate me, me the most, because that's love." she said.

"I just was speaking aloud-" I said.

"I get it, I really do. We usually hate the ones we love, in our own ways. It's that special kind of hate that makes it love." she said, sitting me on the couch. She kissed my twitching cheek, and it stopped twitching.

"That sounds twisted, and disturbing, and-" I said.

"Say it again." she said.

"RAGH! I hate you all, I hate you too, I hate you Mary Jane, because I love you." I said.

She smiled.

"Goddamn, fucking HELL- I DIDN'T NEED THIS!! I NEEDED PEACE!! I NEEDED TO DIE ALONE, OR AT LEAST BY MYSELF!! I CAN'T LIVE, I CAN'T LOVE, I'M TRAPPED!! I'M STUCK!! THERE'S NO WAY OUT AND I JUST WANT IT TO END!!" I said, yelling.

And she said, "I think that's nice. I don't feel the same way, but I'm glad you can let it out."

"But… I… I… Thank you. I don't know why, but that really helped." I said.

"Thought it might. You seem like you've got some repressed Hell in you, and that's really the worst kind. Eventually it ruptures. Do you want me to stay?" she said.

"Yes, yes… I do really like you, and I…" I said.

"You don't need anyone, anything, especially not me. You can shoot to the stars with only your own power. You are the artist, and you can make magic." she said.

I hugged her. I just hugged her.

She hugged me back.

"Acceptance is powerful, and belief can do astounding things. I believe in you." she said.

I asked her if she would like to be my muse again.

"Of course! I get a kick out of it! I wouldn't be doing this if it wasn't fun! Let me get the props-" she said.

"No. I just want to draw you now. Really, you look amazing." I said, and drew her down.

We added it to the portfolio, together.

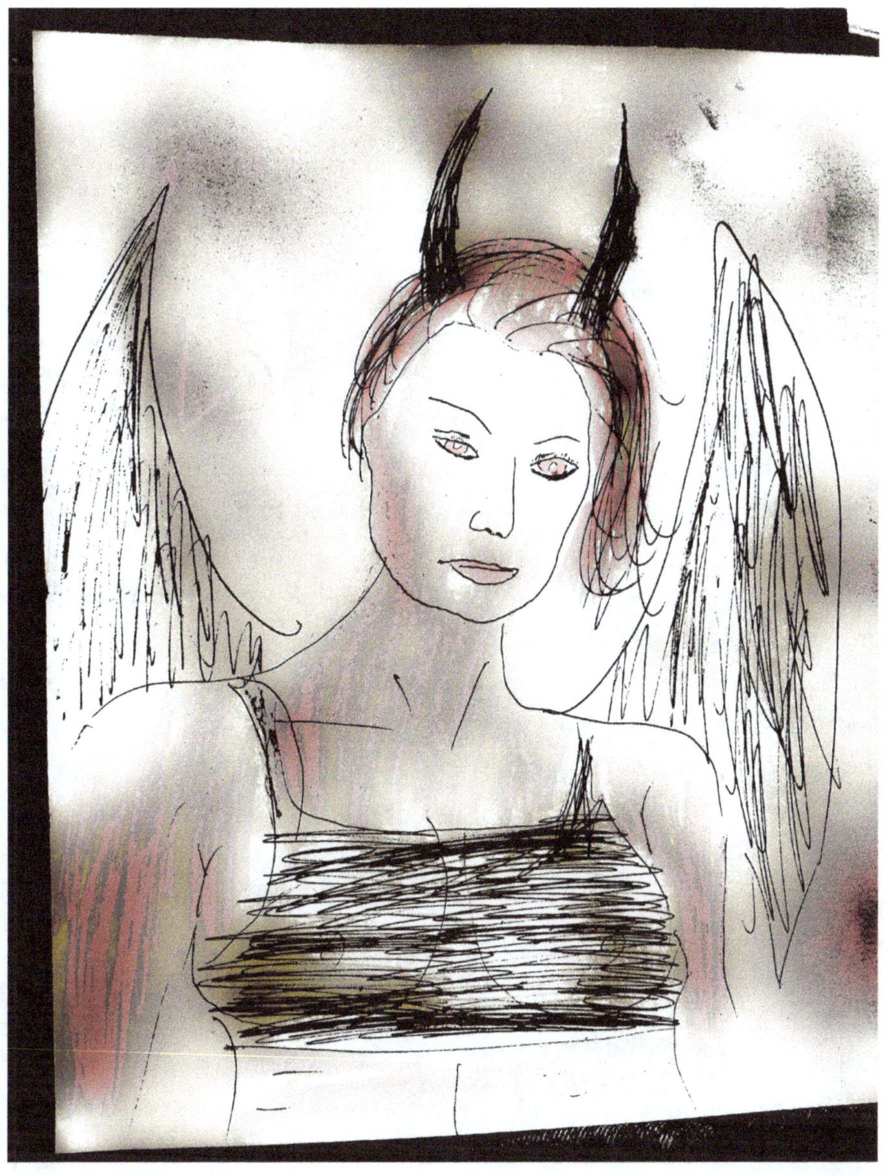

56

Ach, I was being sweet.

I didn't even think that was possible, in truth.

I could ditch him, if I wanted to. I could.

But why should I?

There was no reason to run away in the night, not when I'm having the time of my life.

That was *me* on the cover!! That was *me,* Mary Jane, the Devil's Daughter!! I felt so cool.

Who knows how long it would last? Our relationship? But this portfolio would last the ages. It felt concrete, baked to perfection, like pancakes.

Sure, they may be our own special brand, but we still liked to drizzle on syrup and gorge ourselves.

And fuck, if there's anyone crazier than me, it might be him. I found that oddly comforting. They say birds of a feather flock together… Did they go to the loony bin together, too?

I convinced Luke to see a therapist, eventually. Soon, I hoped. Mine was a real bitch, but I kinda liked her.

She kept on asking me about my past, and I don't think she believed a word of it, but she still gave her own bits of advice.

"Maybe the Devil just needs a stronger hand?" she said.

"Nah, he likes being pushed around, because then he can get in a fight, and then he-" I said.

"Please, continue." she said.

"-He gets you in the end. He always wins, one way or another. He's going to get me, too. Because I am his daughter, and there is no one stronger than my father." I said.

"You sound like you're frightened of him." she said.

"...I am." I said.

"That doesn't sound like a healthy relationship." she said.

"...So? He's family. It's not like I'm going to- I mean, not like I'm gonna- Just leave him? Can I even do that? That sounds mean, and it would teach him a lesson, but he's my dad. He was the only one for me growing up... even though... he stole me from my mother, and... I think he got her to kill herself. You're not recording this, are you?" I said.

"Everything we say is completely between us." she said.

"...But what if he hears this? What if he gets me for this? What if... I know he's listening, and I know he's watching. I know he's waiting, somewhere, just behind the door maybe." I said.

"Hm... It sounds like he makes you very paranoid. No, I don't think he's around the corner. Have you talked to the psychiatrist yet?" she said.

"...He gave me pills, but I don't want to take them in case I overdose." I said.

"You should take your medicine. If it doesn't help, be sure to tell your doctor and they can prescribe something else. It sounds like you've had a very difficult past." she said.

"...You're a bitch. Fuck you." I said.

"...Not a very nice thing to say. Sorry, I will try to be a better listener." she said.

I laughed, and said, "Sorry. Just checking if you were him. He wouldn't say sorry."

She smiled.

"Is it ok that I'm kind of a slut?" I asked her.

"I think it helps if you don't refer to yourself as a derogatory term." she said.

"...But I really am. I just want to fuck, a lot. I was actually thinking of cheating on my artist, for a few days, just to treat myself." I said.

"Your artist?" she said.

"Yeah, he's kinda like my partner. He's a good friend. But I just want to go fuck, y'know? God... That does sound slutty... Maybe I should tell him that?" I said.

"...I think you should be open in your relationships. Not sexually! Just open with your feelings and ideas." she said.

"You think... He'd want to see other people, too, then? I like being his only action, but still... Maybe he should treat himself, too?" I said.

"Is the relationship fulfilling for you?" she asked.

"Yes. But I still feel like cheating. Is it something with how I was raised?" I said.

"...I think a lot of people have those urges. But you have to ask yourself which is more fulfilling, a brief fling, or a steady surge?" she said.

"...Mmm... steady surge, I like that. Sounds nice. You did that on purpose!" I said.

She smiled, and said, "Just a brief nudge. You don't have to tie yourself down if it isn't what you want, but if you find something special in the relationship you should try to build on it, and not throw it out, whether that be with your artist, your dad, or even me. If there is abuse-"

"What?" I said.

"If there is abuse... please, do not continue down this route." she said.

"I kinda told my artist to hate me." I said.

"Does he?" she asked.

"No... I kinda squeezed it out of him. Tempted him into saying it... Do you think he really does?" I said.

"I would ask him that." she said.

"No, he said he didn't... He seems very frustrated, however. I can understand his pain..." I said.

"That's good you are empathetic of others, because that helps you understand yourself better. Perhaps you should take more time for yourself, and allow your relationship to flower by your own hand-" she said.

"I'm just gonna jerk off a lot, then." I said.

"...If you find that helpful, by all means." she said.

I smiled, and she said our minutes were up.

I went home, and thought of that one guy who made me so frustrated, that I broke up with for Luke.

I yelled at him to get off my lawn, because he wasn't coming inside.

He shrugged. Of course. It didn't even matter to him...

I saw my drawing of Luke with the flowers on the fridge.

I smiled to myself.

I texted him, and told him he didn't need to die alone, he didn't need to die at all, and invited him to come over.

Shoot mewled at me

"I just feel trapped, Jane. I'm sorry for yelling." he said at the door.

"It's ok, I know you weren't really yelling at me. Talk to that therapist soon, ok? Mine kinda helped, although I don't trust her motives for it..." I said.

He pet Poopy Star Shoot on my bed.

"You ever get crazy sexual urges?" I said.

"...Um... Yes. But really only for you." he said.

"I nearly cheated on you for a bimbo boy." I said.

"...Oh. Want me to take him... out?" he said.

"How does that make you feel?" I said.

"Like shit. Makes me mad." he said.

"Good, because it didn't happen, and won't. If you didn't care, you'd be the bimbo boy." I said.

"...Ok. You know I would yell and shout, you know I'd even be worse... but there must be a reason for this. Did I do something wrong?" he asked.

"No, you didn't, but I'm not one for a monogamous relationship all the time. Can you understand that?" she said.

"Frankly, I can't. I'd commit, like I'm doing, and not fly away on a fancy..." he said.

"You could be... Hmm... I actually don't know. You could chain me down, have your way with me, and force yourself on me. You wanna do that?" I said.

"...Not really, but I'm open to new experiences." he said.

"...Hm. That's an option, then, for you. Only *you.* You get that, right?" I said.

He perked his eyebrows up, and said, "Well, where did I put the chains... Ah, I got something here. Here you go."

He tossed me a ring from his pocket.

"Stole it from some guy at church, y'know, the one with the frock? That guy. Thought you'd like crap like this." he said.

I giggled.

I put on the chain.

I snickered, as he practically threw himself at me, ripping off my clothes.

He was kissing my neck, an' I said, *"Safe word's... safe word's...* Frantic."

He was strong.

He was lustful.

He bit me at some points.

I lifted up my hooves.

I kissed my chain, my ring... with a cross on it, with my arms around him.

I whispered in his ear, "Frantic."

Mmm... That hit the spot.

Then we smoked cigarettes in my bed.

"You wanna draw our sex?" I asked.

"Nah, I think it's best having people wonder about it, you know, fill in the gaps themselves." he said.

"Hmm… Ok. But people will think of loving with me… after *this* pose… Draw, my artist." I said.

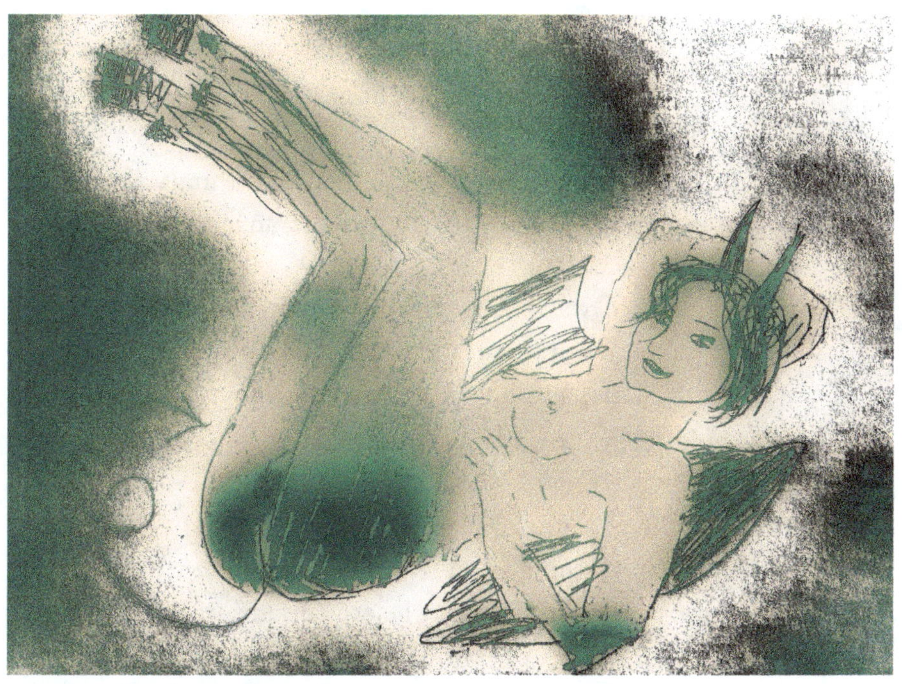

"Now, love me, my artist." I said.
We had only just begun.

57

I think I had my fill of naked women, honestly.

But not my fill of Jane.

We drank together, played music together, and things were great! More than great, perfect! I finally felt at peace, strangely enough, dating Mary Jane.

The portfolio I had was great, with my partner's full support. We were so excited to put it out there, and finally make our names!

"I can finally be Jane, and not the damn *Daughter of the Devil...* Oh, maybe we should put your newspaper refusals in, as well? Give a little backstory?"

"But not even the paper liked them." I said.

"Screw them. If everything good was published, then it'd all be crap. Your stuff is *good.* I mean, it drives me bejesus insane, probably you too, but I think it's great, albeit a little hypocritical of you... Since you do everything you damned, now! Even the most vilest of sins... *groceries.*" she said.

I laughed, "I suppose I just needed to fall in Hell with someone, to realize how foolish I was. Really, you don't invoke any sense of evil in a nonchristian, or maybe a nonreligious person, with your features.

She swished her tail at me, and poked my butt. She said, "Well, yeah. If you look at me from a completely unreligious aspect, I suppose the most I could come up to is some alien phase traveler. Not evil."

"It really was Hell, back home? I mean that as in it sucked." I said.

"Yep! I didn't realize that until I got here, though. You're actually my first decent relationship, since I only dated demons and that bimbo boy." she said.

"You don't... You don't still do anything with the bimbo boy?" I asked.

"I burned his house down, if that's what you're asking. Sucker had it coming, picking on my nun friend, anyway. That was the abusive ex of hers... It's weird how I got her out of that relationship, then fell into her own shit. Stupid of me." she said, starting a cigarette.

"He wasn't the waiter, too? Now that we're connecting the strings?" I asked.

"Nah, that was just some sucker who missed a tip, by *looking down my dress.* Dining and dashing was just an added fuck you." she said.

We went out drinking at a bar we liked, and she wrapped her arms around me, and said, "Look, look there. Let's make BB jealous."

I smiled, as the bimbo boy was glaring at us.

Jane and I kissed, making out at the bar. The bimbo boy shook his head, was about to walk away, but then approached us.

He said to Jane, "I know it was you. I know you're the Devil incarnate. And I'll prove it. BE DAMNED!!"

He splashed her with holy water from a vial in his coat.

She flicked off the holy water, and got up, looking furious.

I hit BB before she could set him on fire, like it looked like she wanted to.

BB took the hit, and tried to grab my collar.

I grabbed him around the head, and threw him to the ground in a judo throw, landing on top of him.

All you really do is use the hip as a torque, and swish, they go onto the ground.

All three of us were expelled from the establishment and banned.

BB yelled at us, as he walked away, calling my girlfriend a filthy slut, and the Devil's Daughter.

I was about to chase after him, but Jane grabbed my arm and held me gently.

She smiled at me, and wiped off the rest of the holy water. "Glad it wasn't acid or something." she said.

"Yeah… People like that make me sick." I said.

We walked home in peace.

Heehee! I was so happy! I could giggle in glee. Luke actually cared for me!

I was actually glad I had fucked bimbo boy, because that was the hottest thing my artist ever did.

I made up for anything I ever did to Luke, and helped him in *multiple* ways, although he actually really liked it when I was on my knees.

He said it was kind of scary as I used my fangs, but I could tell just by feeling that it was exciting for him.

We relaxed, and I smoked a joint after, and my artist was *extra* relaxed.

I heard the Devil in my head sometimes still, but I just kissed my stolen Christian ring, and laughed at the Devil.

The burns from the pentagram hurt awfully, but the marijuana helped dull the pain.

We watched some silly old show, some damned old comedians in black and white. Luke would probably know who they were, but I didn't give a shit.

Maaan… As the marijuana hit me, I never felt it could be *so* deep. This humor… this person beside me… Maaan. I felt like I must've missed the Earth and wound up in Heaven instead, when I got to this point.

Shit. I started seeing things. This crap was probably laced with something, since I got it from the "weird" drug dealer of mine… There were classy ones, there were ghetto ones, and then there was the weird one.

Shit. Bats don't belong in the apartment. Shoo, bats, shoo.

My artist didn't seem to see them, so I guess I was hallucinating. He just wrapped an arm around me and we snuggled together.

All my old demons were harassing me, the ones I fucked and soon got bored of, or who were only trying to add an extra layer of torment on me.

I sat with my artist, Luke, as they surrounded me, calling me names.

One of them got too close, and made me jump.

Luke asked me, "Are you ok, Jane?"

"Never better! L-Let's turn on more lights." I said.

I held his hand as he turned on all the lights in the apartment.

"You're not gonna be one of them, are you?" I asked Luke, as I saw Bimbo Boy in my mind's eye, splashing me with something that would actually hurt me, or maybe pulling out a switchblade on me instead.

"Hm? No, these guys are all wimps, anyway. They stay in the shadows." Luke said.

The demons hissed at Luke.

"Oh. You can see them. Yeah, th-that o-one over there is the scariest." I said, pointing at one with dark eyeshadow, pale skin, and three arms.

"Why would you date that guy?" Luke asked.

"I-I don't know, now. Three arms? Who else has three arms?" I said.

The pale, three armed clown snickered at me.

"Want me to draw them? You can burn the pics." Luke said.

"Oh. Yes, let's do that." I said.

I wrapped myself under my artist's arm, as he drew the clown monster demon.

That demon did look kind of silly, as I saw him in the light on paper.

I lit it in flames in my hand, and my old boyfriend disappeared.

We did this one by one for the demons, and soon it was only us two again.

We watched the comedians, Abbott and Costello, yeah, and I decided to not smoke so much pot anymore.

59

I held the knife over my wrist. I could do it... Like in the past...

But I really didn't feel like it so much, anymore. I was the artist, Luke, and I had a great gal and an up and coming career.

I listened to Knockin' on Heaven's Door again. I wondered if they were even accepting artists?

I closed the pocket knife knife part, and used the bottle opener of it instead, to open another beer.

Ahh... I looked back at all the pictures of Jane, smiling to myself and drinking a beer. Jane really looked different, in a different sort of way, just because I knew her story now.

Oh, shit. Jane said she'd be here soon. I reopened the knife part and began sharpening colored pencils.

She hummed as she walked inside, locking up behind her.

Poopy Star Shoot, although I jokingly called him Rasputin, was sleeping on the couch.

Jane had moved in.

We thought if we could be partners in art, partners in love, then we may as well up it up a notch and live together. I'd be seeing a therapist soon, but I worried about that...

Maybe they'd tell me every new, good life choice of mine was crazy.

I drew someone else, as Jane was making tea.

He looked a little like me... a lot like someone I knew... and a lot like- I couldn't really place it.

But if I looked just hard enough at him... I saw him look back.

And I heard the voice in my head, but no voice I've ever heard before. I knew it was mine somehow...

"We are all the master.

"I have taken on a role in my life. I have taken on being the master of these words and fiction, this art and plot.

"I have taken on my own destiny.

"So this is a friendly reminder from the writer...

"Take the words in your own hands, and bring about fate yourself."

I wrote these words down, and signed my name. From the artist.

Then Jane and I got back to work. We had so much more to do!

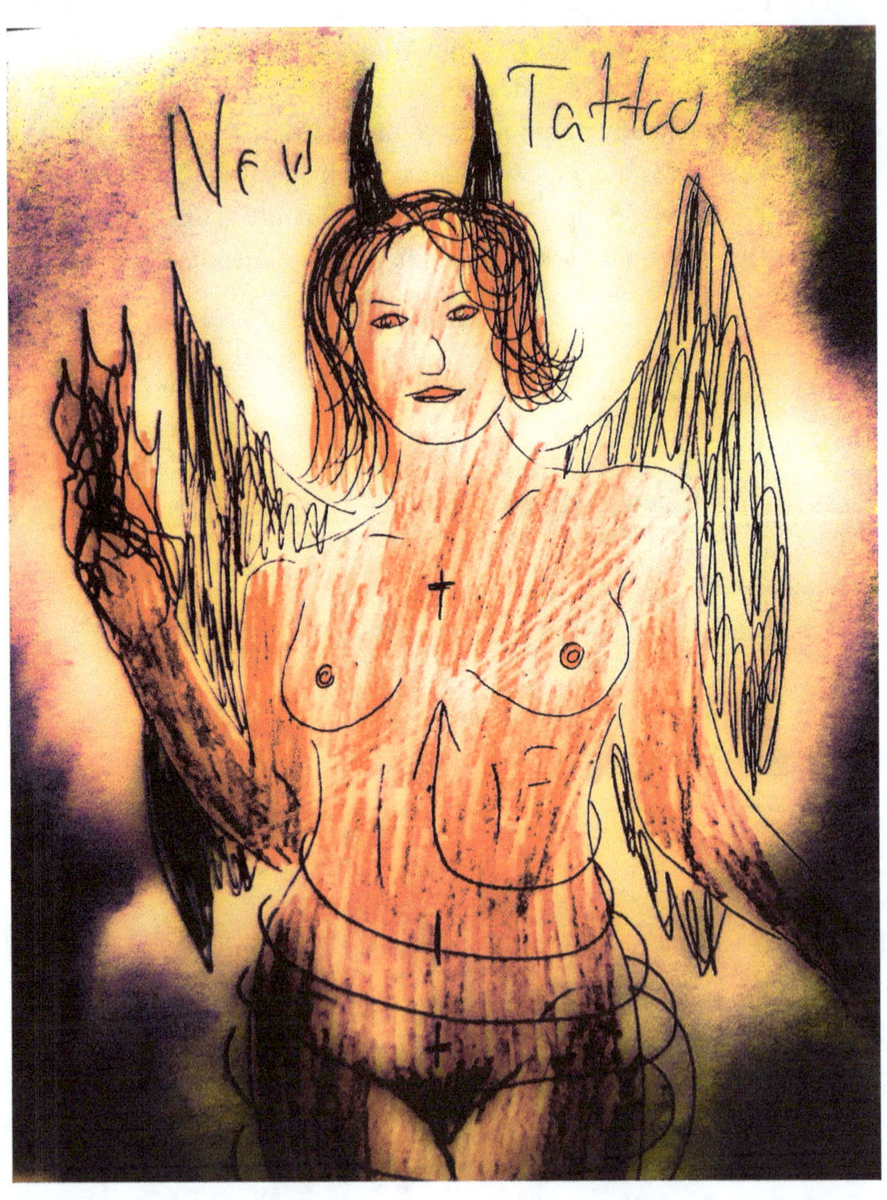
New Tattoo

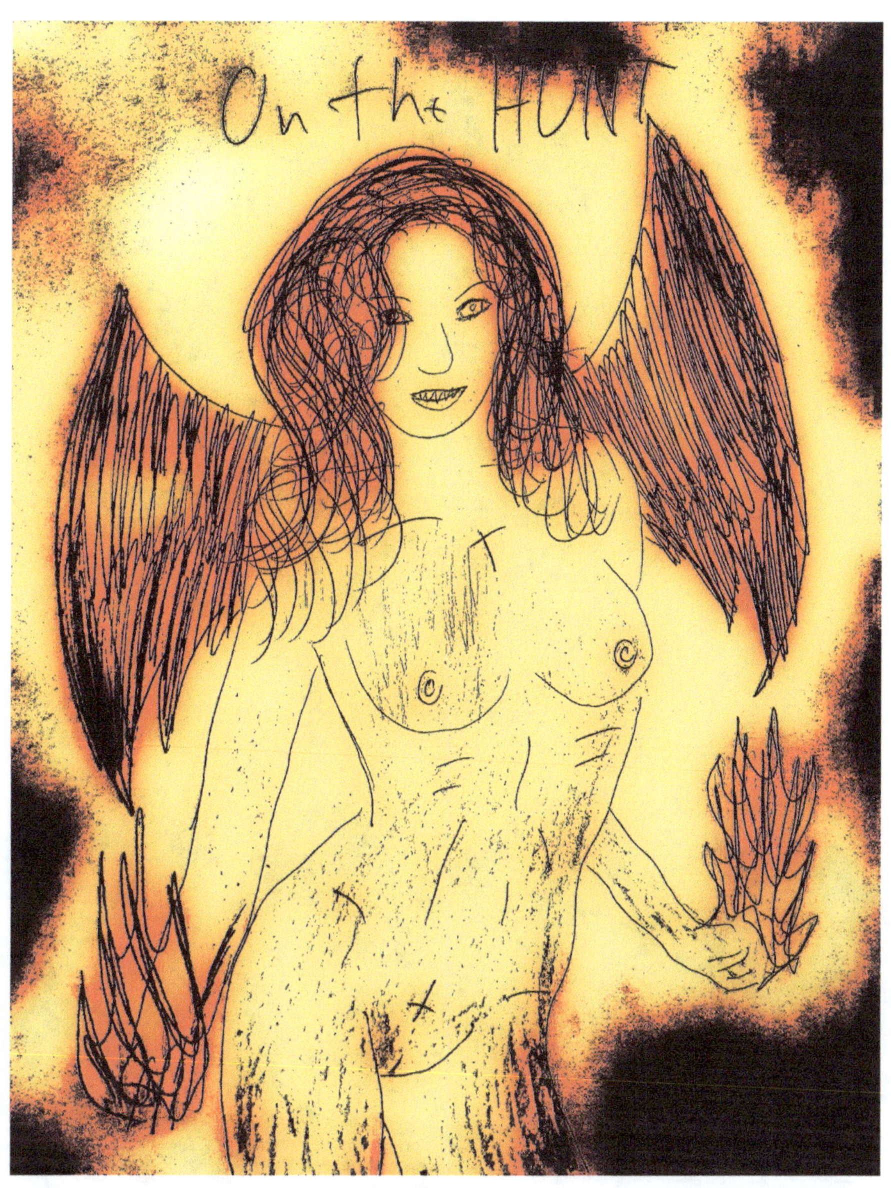
On the HUNT

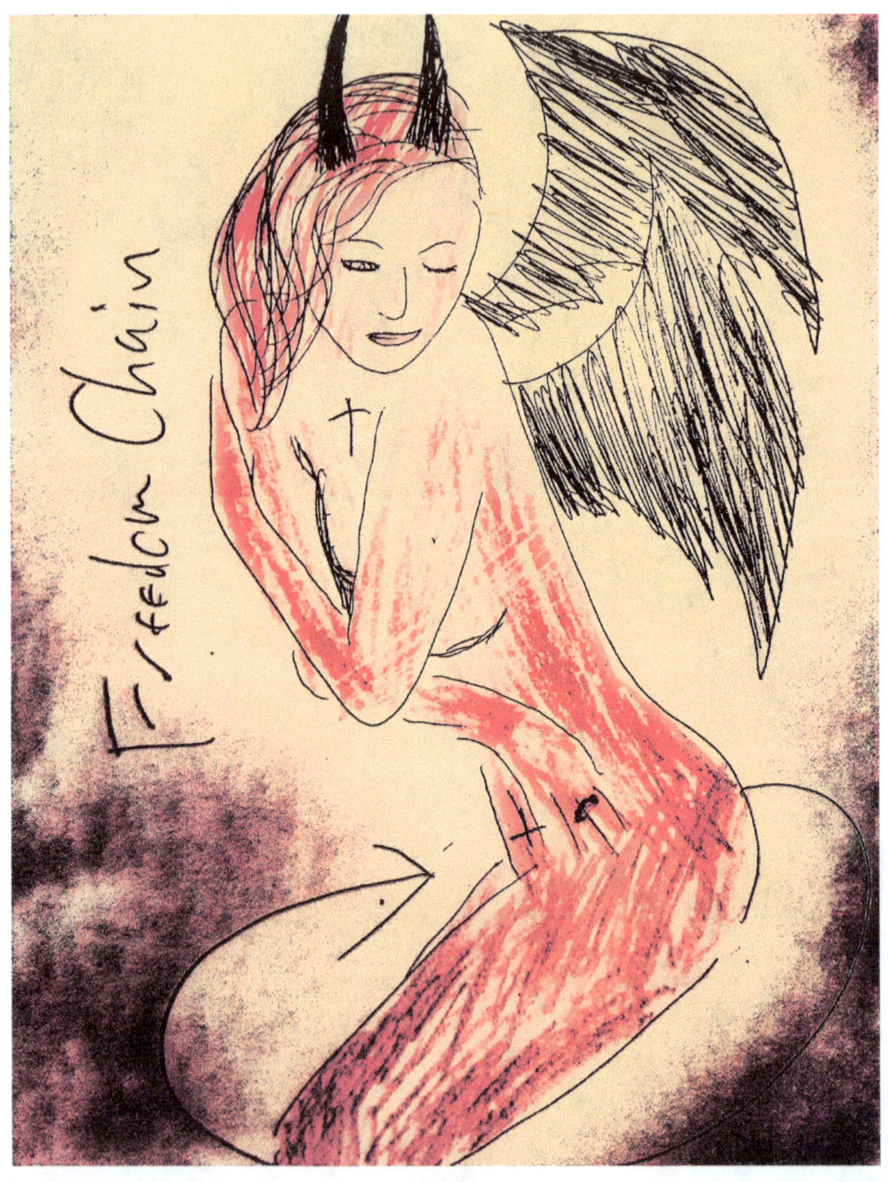
Freedom Chain

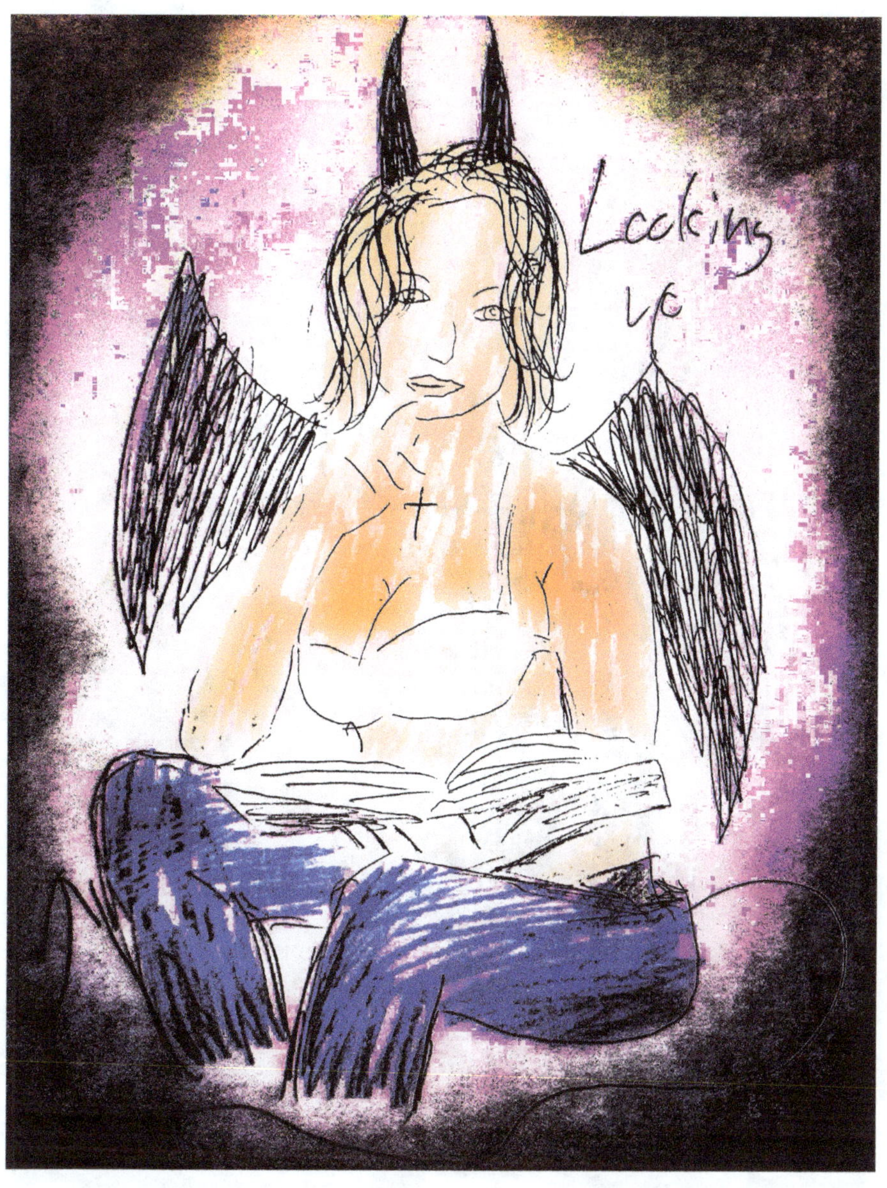
Looking
up

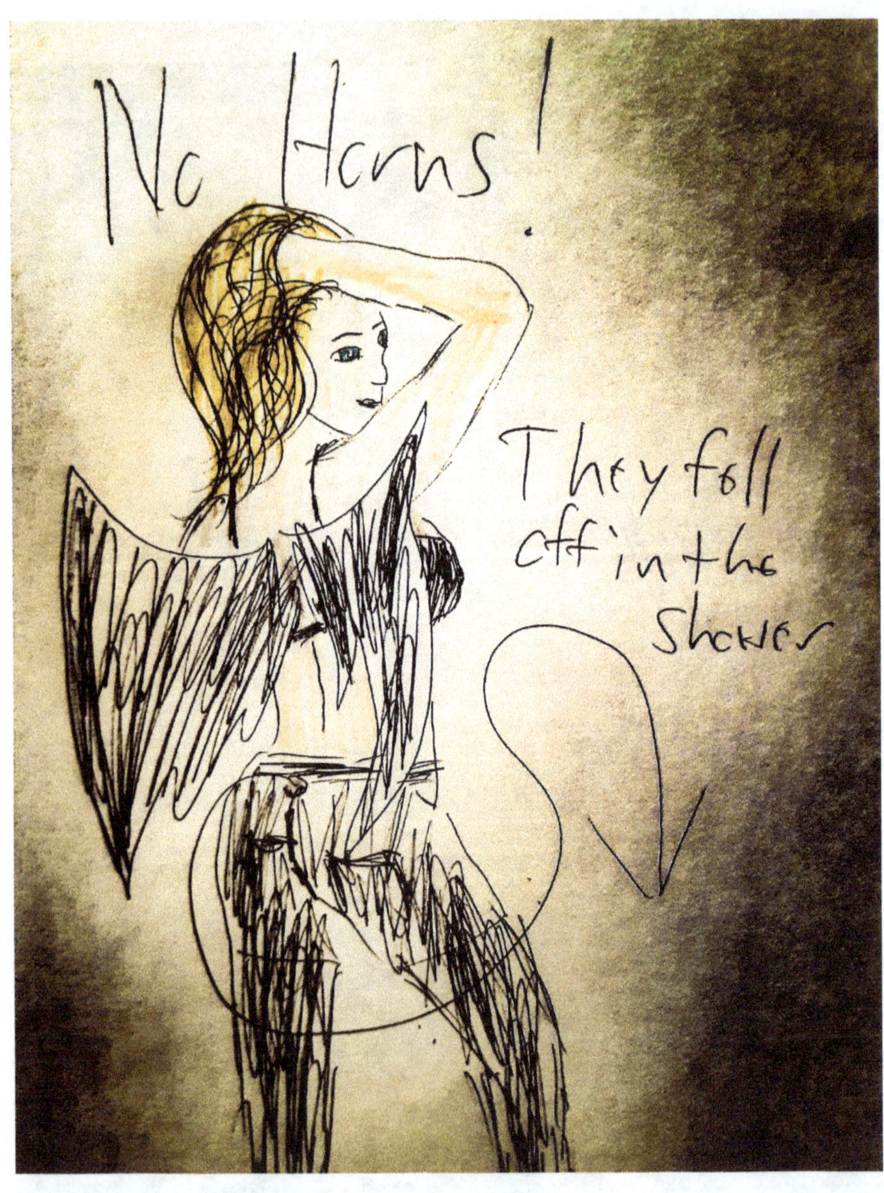
No Horns!
They fell
off in the
shower

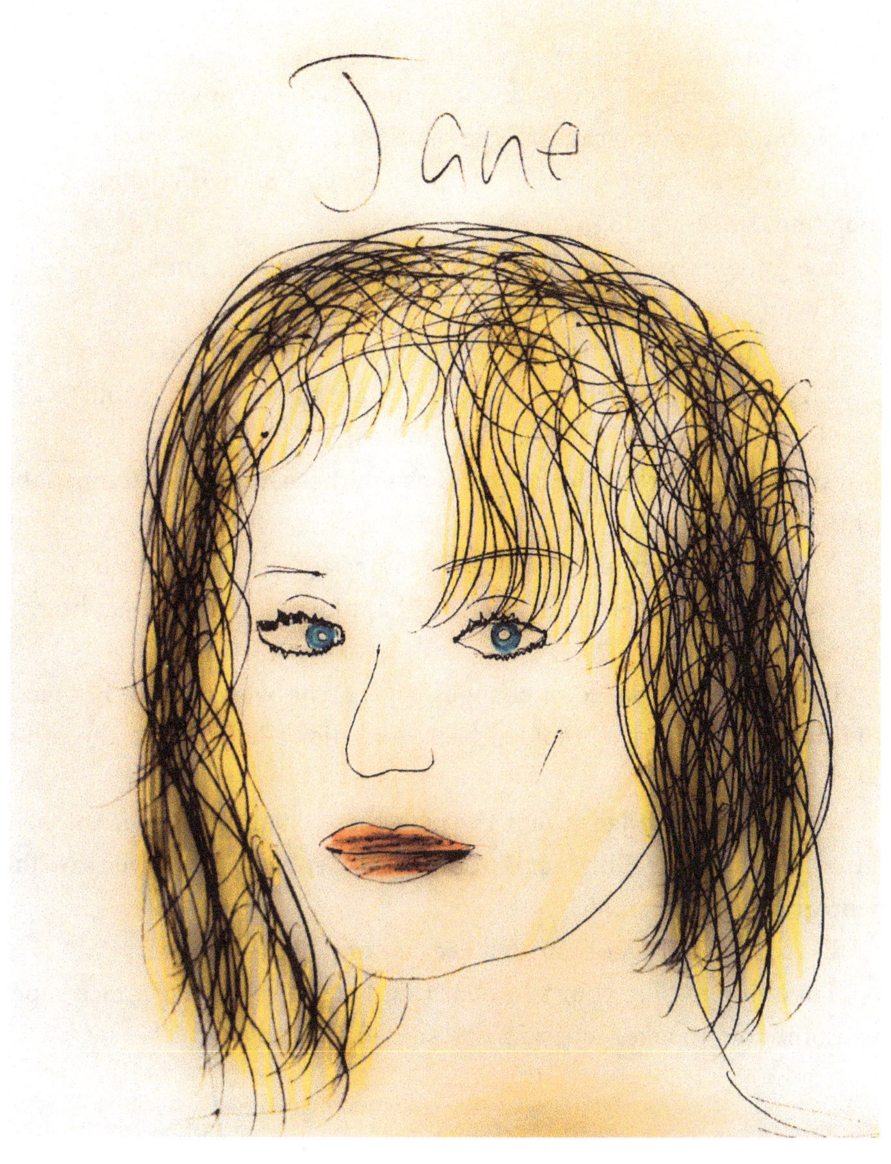
Jane

60

"I heard you when you said you wanted to die. You said you wanted to kill yourself by lung cancer." she said to me.

I gulped, as I was smoking my pipe. Then I started coughing, and coughing, and coughing.

Jane got me a cup of coffee, as I continued to hack a lung.

"I want you to-" she was saying.

"I want to quit. Thanks for reminding me of that." I said.

"That's really the secret. You have to want to do it, not be told to not do it by someone else." Jane said and smiled.

I smiled, and flicked the last bit of ash in the ashtray, and dumped the ashtray in the trash.

"You can clean up all the tobacco crumbs and ash remnants later. I'm so proud of you!" Jane said, smiling in happiness... with normal human teeth.

Those were the weirdest changes, and the hooves, because her teeth and hooves just sort of molded back, and didn't fall off like the other parts...

I wondered why Jane went through these changes. Was it the new tattoo she got? The Christian Cross on the pentagram? I never saw the pentagram ever again.

She seemed happier than Hell because of it, quite honestly.

"I'm going to take your soul, but first I'm going to have a nice super awesome soul to take." she said, and smiled.

I could tell she tried to swish her tail, cuz she did a little hip move-ment.

But she didn't have a tail.

"Er, I was gonna stroke your cheek or something. I feel awkward." Jane said, looking back at her behind.

I still snuck off to get cigarettes. It was just... madness, and dealing with the dual madness of voices and addiction was Hell.

I saw Jane smoking a cigarette when I got home, but she flicked it away to hide it.

I lit up a cigarette in front of the apartment, as she sat on the bench.

She giggled.

"Oh well. We can figure it out later. Let's do something really stupid and sappy or our next pose, ok?" she said.

"Why? I thought you didn't like that stuff." I said.

"I don't, but I'm feeling... well I'm feeling it'll be appropriate." she said.

She got dressed in some lingerie, and I drew her, trying to make the "Love" banner she was holding come out nice.

I nearly finished the drawing-

But then tackled her in a hug, and we wrestled on the floor, laughing.

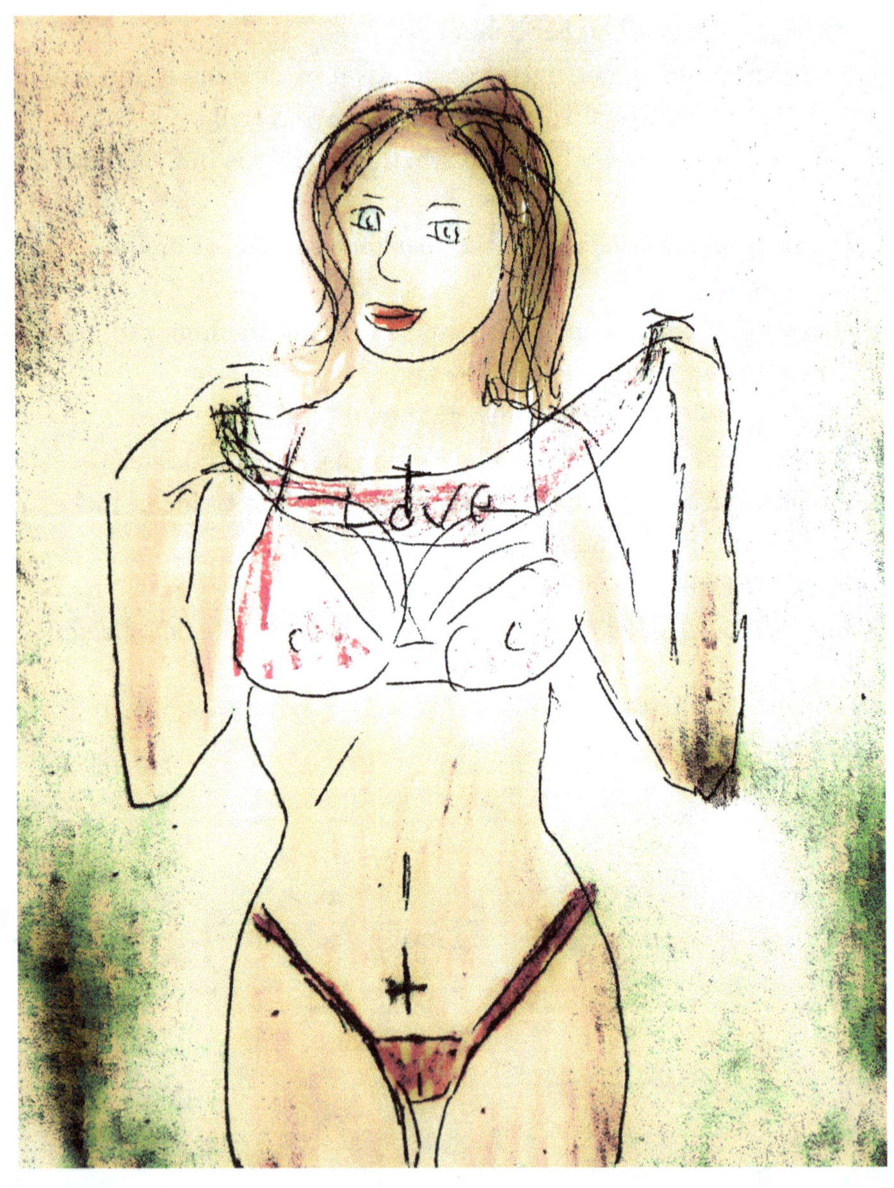
Love

<h1 style="text-align:center">61</h1>

You've changed on the outside... but look at yourself on the inside.

I stared at the mirror, and I saw myself as a demon.

I was different now! The changes proved I was different now!

But the devil me smirked, and said, "You were always this in the end."

I screamed, and threw the mirror to the floor, where it smashed into tons of devil mes, laughing at my foolishness.

Luke saw the whole thing, and asked, "...Are you ok?"

I turned to him in fury, and said, *"No! I was never ok! I'll always-* Erghm... I'll always be a bitch really."

"...Wanna smash more mirrors? We can. I'm sure our luck will be terrible, but whatever." he said.

"No... That does sound fun, but no..." I said, sighing and starting a cigarette.

Luke drew me something as I smoked.

"Here, a little angel you. For luck." he said.

I smiled, taking the little me. Here was someone who saw who I was.

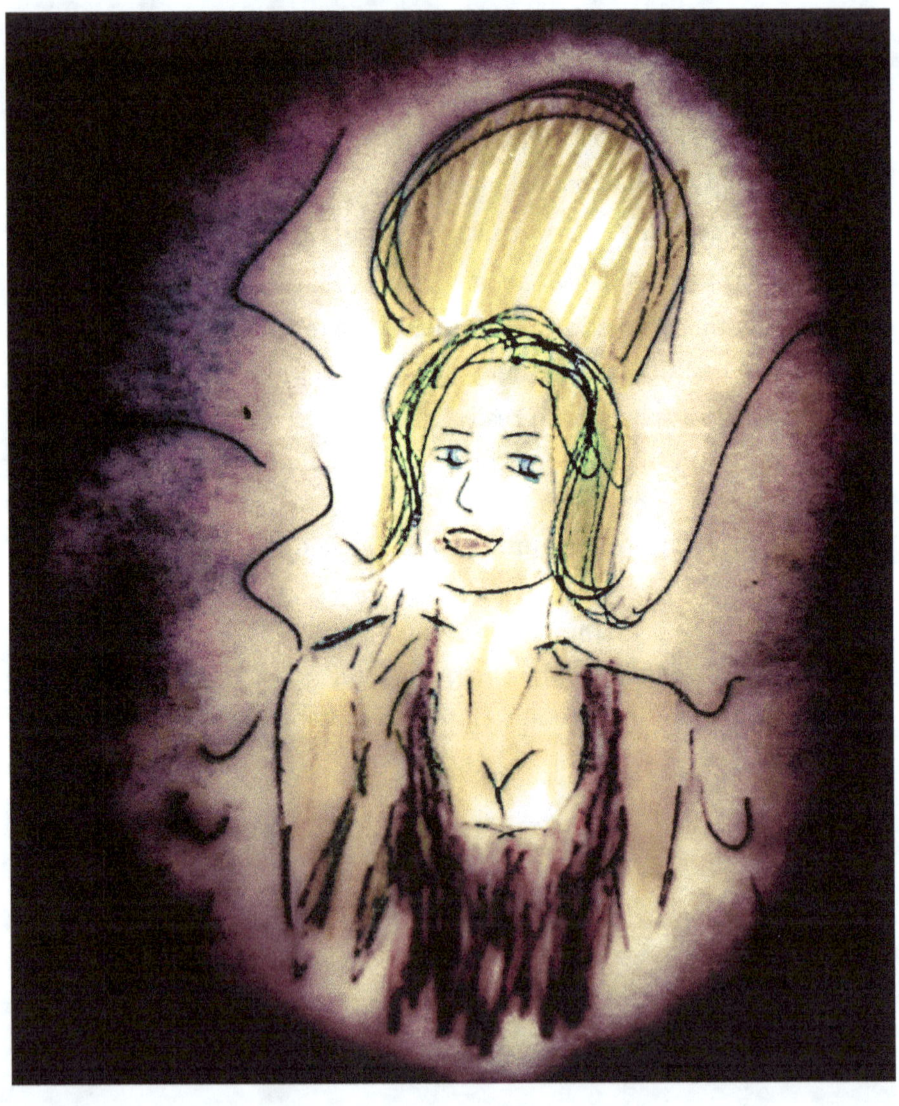

62

WHO AM I REALLY-

WAIT. DON'T LOOK AT ME.

DON'T SCREAM AT ME-

DON'T YELL AT ME-

I WANT TO SHOUT AT YOU-

I'm sorry.

...THAT'S VERY NICE THAT YOU FEEL THAT WAY. I think I can calm down now. It's nice that you have a nice relationship, even if it might be brief. You have a nice love, who even if is evil incarnate, is a good person, in her own way. That's all we ever really look for.

Yes, we do look for that, don't we?

HAHA. Yes. It is better to find love and lost, than none at all.

Why do you think I'm going to lose her?

BECAUSE SHE NEVER WAS HERE.

SHE WAS ALWAYS THE DEVIL'S DAUGHTER- You know what, you're right. Maybe it'll last. Sorry. I'm a little pessimistic. Just relax, and don't listen to me so often, ok?

Ok. See ya, voice. Come back sometime-

I'LL TRADE OFF FOR THE NEXT ONE. There's tons of voices in your head... but you don't notice us all all the time. A million voices call-ing... All for you. Take on the worst one while you can.

So, I started a cigarette, and talked to Satan himself.

His eye was twitching.

"Why are you talking to me? Summon me right, and we can talk. Correctly." Satan said.

I put on some Devil music.

"Why would you listen to me? I'm the Devil." he said.

"Because I've always heard you before. You were the worst influence." I said.

"Only cuz the music you listened to." the Devil said.

"Nah... I think it was Catholic school which really allowed me to meet you. Every horrible thing... was you." I said.

"I'm glad you see it that way. All that pestering, hate, and evil-" he said.

"But I don't care. I don't believe in you." I said.

"But you're talking to me now. Really. This is the Devil, really." he said.

"I still don't believe it. I'm... a little more grounded." I said.

The Devil frowned, and said, *"I am proud of you. I'm glad you could date my daughter... for she will be your biggest regret-"*

"Ah, Goddamnit. Fuck off, BahGod, every metal lyric I listened to showed the pride of MAN. Not you. We are all together, us, and not you. Why don't you just get out of my life? Leave us be." I said.

The Devil snickered, and bowed.

"For you, dear artist, may we meet again. As father and son?" he said.

I threw my beer at him, and he vanished.

Why did I ever listen to the Devil?

Jane came back home with a case of beer, and sat on my lap.

Was I the worst voice in my head, instead?

63

It's getting too dark to see.

And I feel the Devil in my bed.

Has this ever happened?

Or is this just my own Hell?

I woke up, and hugged Luke. He was still sleeping beside me.

I yawned, stretched, and listened to the birds chirp from the opened window.

"Kill yourself, Jane." a bird whispered.

I smiled at the birds. Hearing voices was silly.

It was all the Devil, in the end...

I ate cereal, after it crackled under the milk.

I felt the intrusive thought of my dad feeling my-

Man! This cereal was so good!

"Morning, Luke." I said, as my artist got up from bed, walking into the kitchen nude.

"Morning, Jane. How are you? Taking your meds?" Luke said.

I nodded and smiled, saying, "This new shit should be good for me. You know that other crap really wonked me out, though, so I'm thinking this will be a better change of pace."

"Ok. I only take one injection, nowadays. But keep cool, and don't be afraid to try something new!" Luke said, and smiled.

I smiled back, as the other scars I had seemed to be opened up, hurting, even though most have faded by now.

I sighed, and said, "Y'know, Luke... There are some things I don't want to tell you about my past. Painful things. Can you understand that?"

He looked sadly at me, and said, "I just don't want you to hurt any-more."

"The only reason my dad- hurt me... was to make me stronger." I said.

"That sounds like it hurt." he said.

I gulped.

I wanted to wonder at Luke. He must be someone- something- not from here, like me. That would make him more relatable to me.

But I knew he was completely human. They really are strange, odd, wonderful creatures, humans.

I was glad I was at least half of one of them.

"I... I want to finish my cereal." I said.

"Want any eggs?" he said.

"...Maybe." I said.

Luke cooked some eggs and bacon on the stove.

I finished the cereal and ate the second breakfast.

Now was where I should... should tell him about my dream. Yeah. "I had a nightmare." I said.

"What was it about?" he asked.

"It was what you and I do. But my Dad was watching. Eventually he and you switched places, and you were watching... and enjoying it." I said.

He looked sick.

He said, "...I think you watch too much porn, Jane. That sounds frankly very disturbing."

"It felt like it was real." I said.

I cried, and Luke hugged me immediately.

I cried on his shoulder.

I expected him *to whisper like my Dad did-*

But Luke said, "I'm here for you, Jane."

"Can I dream in your head tonight? I don't like being by myself." I said.

"Yes. I forgot you could do that, actually." he said.

"Sometimes I can... but... Sometimes dreams take advantage of you, and you think you're the one in charge... but they turn the tables. It's very difficult to get ahold of a good dream." I said.

"I think we should enjoy the day, for now. We can work on it later. How is the theater going?" Luke asked.

"I love it. At first I just helped the crew, but now that I'm one of them, it feels even better." I said.

We kissed each other before we left each other for the day, and I went to the theater.

I laughed and enjoyed myself! We were all nude! We got great reviews, so far, and if we kept this up we'd eventually really become class act performers.

Eventually I went back home, as Luke got back.

He sighed, saying he had a rather bad day.

We talked about it, and he admitted that some of his family was in the dumps.

We went to bed, and just slept off the exhaustion.

I clutched him close, and made sure to jump into his head before someone else could jump into mine.

He was sitting on a chair and waiting for me, in this dream.

"I'd never do something so sinister as watch you get raped, Jane. We're in my dream, now, and all I can tell you is... You don't have to suffer."

It was just a blank space, with him on a chair.

"It's very open in here." I said.

"This is my canvas. It's always open, so open even the rats get in..." he said. Some rats scurried past his feet, very cute rats albeit.

He took out a cigarette and smoked it.

"My brother was born in the year of the rat. So these little guys really aren't that evil to me." he said.

The rats danced before him, and somehow, one of them winked at me.

"He's a good guy. This is my little bro." my artist said, and picked up the winking rat.

"...What's he do?" I asked.

"Oh, just live his life. He's very stubborn, independently stubborn. I'll let him get back to being a vegan." Luke said, and let the rat scamper away.

The rat turned into a raccoon, and did a somersault, just for me.

I clapped for the raccoon, and the raccoon bowed, and scampered away to dumpster dive.

"My other brother was born in the year of the dragon." he said.

"Dragon? That sounds scarier than a rat." I said.

The dragon flew over us, right over our shoulders. It was completely made of metal, and screeched in roaring beauty.

"He likes to rap." Luke said.

The metal dragon started his own beat with his wings, and rapped for us, and Luke and I danced. Eventually he flew away, and we listened to the dragon in the distance.

"My sister was born in the year of the horse. She's a rather wild one." Luke said.

A horse galloped before me, and allowed me to ride her.

Luke watched as I rode the wild horse, and the horse had a spider on her shoulder.

I pet the black widow, and the spider laughed.

I was soon exhausted from riding the horse, and she let me get off gently, and I waved the spider and the horse goodbye, as they ran off to school.

"I was born in the year of the dog. I will always be beside you, like some damn mutt." Luke said.

He turned into a huge wolf.

"I was always from the lupine aspect. I feared them before, for what they represented in my mind… but they are only me." Luke the wolf said, and howled.

I stroked his fur, and we watched the full moon rise above us, him beside me, keeping me safe.

We woke up in the middle of the night, to the full moon from the open window, and hugged each other, both human.

64

I drew Luke in his lupine form.

"Bowwow, babe. You look good with all this fuzz." I said, finishing my drawing.

"Even though I shaved my head?" he said.

"Especially since you shaved your head. You still got a beard, though." I said, admiring my wolf Luke drawing.

He looked at it, and said, "...Not bad. Why aren't you the artist, instead of me??"

"Oh, quit flattering, vile he beast. I'm not that good…" I said.

"...Seriously. You make even better shit than I do!" Luke said.

"Ach, this is your thing. I just do it as a hobby, ever since you inspired me." I said.

"...I don't know… What if we-" he said.

"Nonono. I prefer this role, as the muse. It's a lot less stressful." I said.

"...Ok. I can get that." he said.

I hung up my drawing on the fridge, and set off for the day.

Luke was still staring at his lupine self, as I left.

The cat was air pawing on the couch, having a good dream. Stupid cat.

I got home to Luke crying to crying to Knockin' on Heaven's Door.

I quickly asked him if he was alright.

He said, "I just… my old cat. I'm sad for him… I know, that's stupid, and lame-"

I said, "I don't think that's lame."

"He was a good guy, and he had such a shitty life in his old home... I gave 'im a good home.... And he died from FLEAS. I FEEL... so sad..." Luke said, as the tears streamed down his face.

"You said he was an old cat when you got him. It's ok." I said.

"I don't want to show this weakness, this heartrending weakness-" he said.

"I don't think it's weak. I'm glad you can accept this strength, this sadness." I said.

"Thank you. Well. Let's drink." he said, wiping off the tears.

Poopy Star Shoot rubbed against my artist, and we drank.

I put the cat in Luke's arms after I picked him up, and Shoot purred like a baby.

"Babies don't purr." Luke said after I told him that.

"This one does!" I laughed, and smiled.

Shoot seemed to be smiling as we cuddled him together.

I smiled as he drew the mysticalness of the feline with its damn tongue out.

He was just a cat. A stupid cat.

But I loved him. I loved them both.

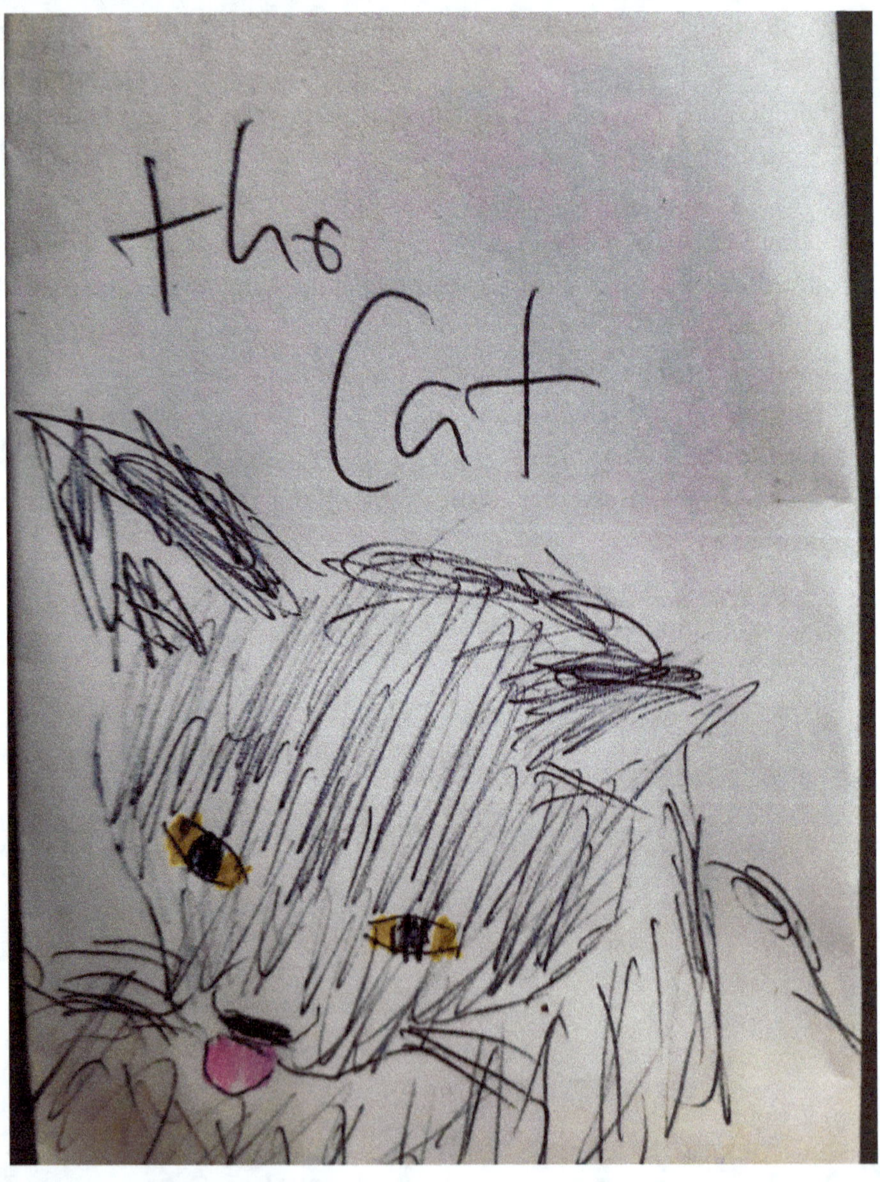
the
Cat

65

All three of us decided to get out of this damn town, Luke, the cat, and I.

I'd say we drove off into the sunset, happily ever after...

But we both know that's not how stories really end.

They continue, until y'know, we die, cut short.

Probably randomly getting hit by a car.

Or slipping in the shower.

Or eating a bad rat.

Those three things happened to us, before we left in the morning, all coincidentally...

And we were stuck with a choice while we were trapped in limbo.

Would we go up? Down? Or just stay here?

The cat pet us, in his natural god form, and left to continue his life, another life.

So it was only Luke and I.

"At least we're together." I said.

"Yes, together forever, actually... dead. I love you, Mary Jane, my muse." Luke said.

"I love you too, Luke, my artist." I said.

We walked off into the shrouds of death, to enjoy our eternity, hand in hand.

And then an angel appeared before us, to give us a lift.

66

"I'd say that was a rather good finisher." my angel said, "But now is where we come out of the haze."

I smiled to my guardian angel, and said, "Morning- Afternoon- Evening? Hello, Yule."

Yule said, "Heya, Luke! I hope this was a fulfilling artsy plot for you! It made *me* happy, if anything."

Jane was pale at the sight of Yule's pale albino skin, and said, "Y-You're beautiful."

"I think you're cute, too!" Yule said, shaking Jane's hand, "Yule. Yule Tidings."

"Merry Christmas?" Jane said.

Yule laughed, and said, "You're a cool cat, Jane. I like what you did in the poses! It's hard to get a good pose out of someone."

"...So we're really dead? I thought I'd go to Hell..." Jane said.

Yule shrugged, with her hands in her pockets, and said, "Nah. You had a horrible life! God is especially nice to you folk, poor demons in Hell... C'mon. We've got better things to do. Like come back to the fold... You've been in life for so long, I think you can have another go, for a little bit longer."

Yule smiled, snapped her fingers, and I awoke in the hospital.

Mary Jane was in the next bed over, with a bandage over the gash on her forehead.

We laughed, looking at each other, and she got up to hug me as my whole body was in a cast.

She woozily tripped onto me, and fell into a kiss with me.

And the nurses let us kiss, even though we looked far from beautiful, in complete utter pain, but together.

We spent a while recuperating, but eventually got back to-

My landlord finally was able to kick me out.

"You and that lady, all the time! Doing some sort of disgusting FILTH! No, I've finally found a clause in your lease, that makes it impossible for you to come back!" he said.

"But… you wrote the clause." I said.

"And I changed the locks, too! Your shit is on the curb." he said, slamming the door in my face.

We got to the curb and big trucks had just loaded up my stuff and drove away with it.

"B-But… my pictures, my drawings, everything we had…" I said.

"I sent it in. That was the last thing I did, before I y'know, fell into the brink. Be thankful for the landlord, because if he wasn't so pissed about the running water, I'd actually be dead…" Jane said.

We walked to the pancake place, as the sun was setting, and I drew her again after we sat down, with her gash scar on her forehead.

"Coffee?" she asked.

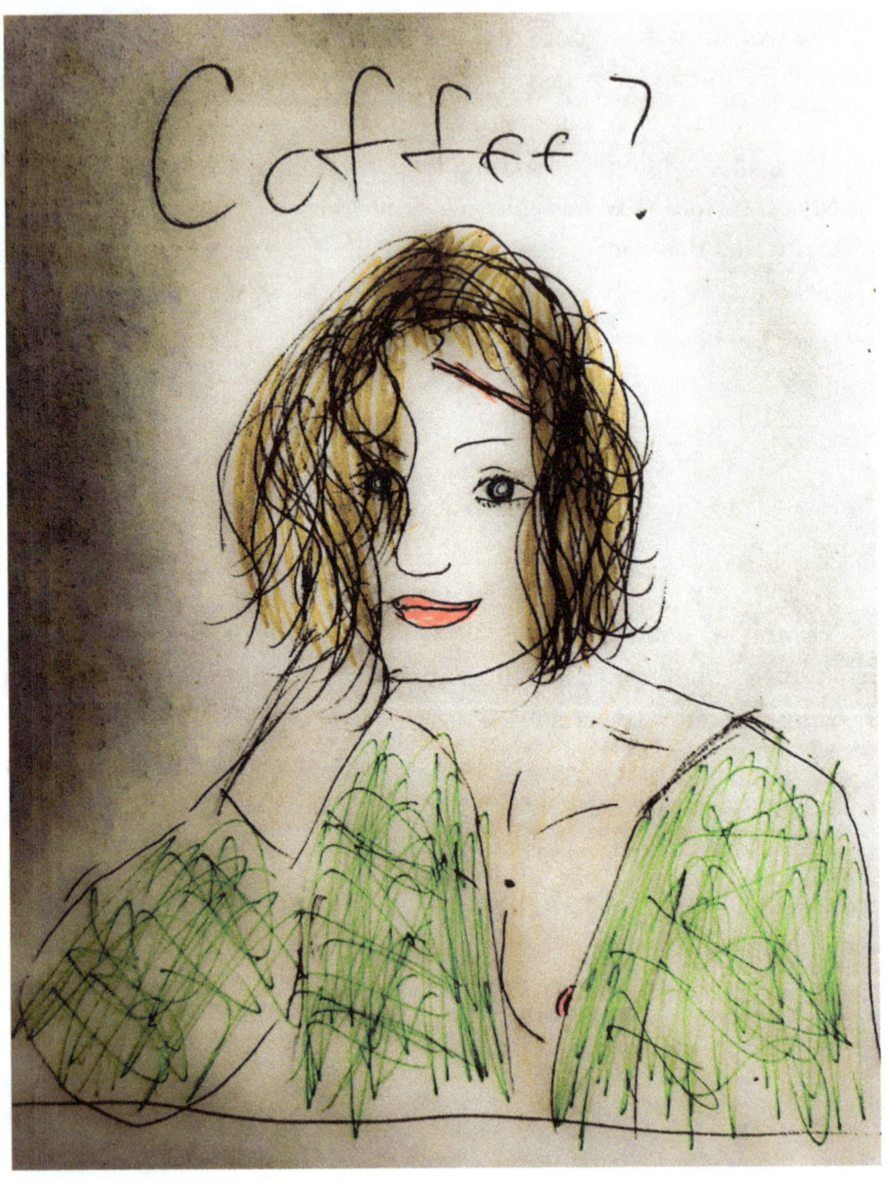

The end of life isn't an end, and it doesn't have to be...
The End